Croquet

The Complete Guide to History, Strategy, Rules and Records

The Complete Guide to History,

Croquet

Strategy, Rules and Records

by James Charlton & William Thompson

Illustrations by Katherine Freeman
Photographs by Roger Adler
Book and cover design by Andrew Bromberg

TURTLE PRESS

•

CHARLES SCRIBNER'S SONS

New York • New York

Library of Congress Catalog Card Number 76—56089
ISBN 0—916844—01—3
ISBN 0—916844—00—5 pbk.

Library of Congress Cataloging in Publication Data

Charlton, James M   1939—
   Croquet.

   Bibliography: p. 173
   1. Croquet. I. Thompson, William G., 1932—
joint author. II. Title.
GV931.C44   796.35'4   76—56089
ISBN 0—916844—01—3
ISBN 0—916844—00—5 pbk.

We would like to thank the following:

G.N. Aspinall, Ted Prentis, H.B. Swope Jr., S. Joseph Tankoos, Margaret Hope, John Jaques, New York Croquet Club, Mary Alma Yousey, Mrs. Moss Hart, Library of Congress, United States Croquet Association, New York Public Library, Mrs. W. Dickenson, Katherine Freeman, and a particular thanks to Jack Osborn.

Contents

FOREWORD

The croquet game most of us remember has grown and changed for the better over the years until it has evolved into an even more stimulating and competitive form combining the physical and mental challenge of golf, billiards and chess.

Many people adept at more strenuous sports have taken up croquet as a second or third activity. Both youthful and middle-aged players have developed a keen interest in the game, and it is the primary outdoor recreation for many.

To date the game's greatest weakness in the USA has been the lack of reliable, non-conflicting information regarding where and how it should be played, by what rules as well as their origins. Now, in the following pages, you can finally get these answers and much more about this great game.

This long needed book by Jim Charlton and Bill Thompson fills a huge vacuum in the literature on croquet in America and marks a pivotal point in the resurgence of interest in the game. Along with the many fascinating, frustrating and amusing aspects of croquet, you will also learn herein of the skill gap which exists between our better equipped and organized English friends and America's best players. There is a challenging opportunity for our current backyard players to move up the skill scale and discover the truly interesting nuances of the American game by adopting the techniques and rules advanced by the members of the United States Croquet Association.

While far too many to mention in this preface, there are nonetheless a few prime contributors who should be noted. Each successful group (or club) must be sparked by the catalystic efforts of one or two key leaders such as the late John Lavalle and Milton 'Doc' Holden of Southampton; the late John David Griffin and Neda Ted Prentis of the Westhampton Mallet Club; Archie Peck and Andy Fuller of The Palm Beach Croquet Club; Herbert Bayard Swope Jr. and the late S. Joseph Tankoos of the New York Croquet Club; the leaders of the West Coast and Bermuda groups and lastly:

the English and World Champions John W. Solomon and G. Nigel Aspinall whose unflagging generosity provided hands-across-the-sea inspiration. Without the considerable efforts of all of these, modern American croquet (let alone this book) simply would not be.

To those families, individuals and/or clubs currently playing the old 9 wicket/2 stake Double Diamond game, we urge you to try the more sophisticated six wicket version and become better prepared to compete with others in the growing list of U.S. Croquet Association clubs.

Similarly, to those beginners interested in forming a croquet club in your area, we extend an invitation to apply for membership in the U.S. Croquet Association.

Jack R. Osborn, President
United States Croquet Association
635 Madison Avenue, New York, New York

BOSTON.
PUBLISHED BY G. D. RUSSELL & COMPANY, 126 TREMONT, OPP. PARK ST.

INTRODUCTION

Croquet is a sport that many people have played at one time or another in their lives. Most of us are familiar with the garden variety game with wire hoops, few rules, and a layout that is as varied as the people who play. In reality, however, croquet is an extremely difficult sport, requiring intense concentration and detailed knowledge of shots and strategy. Those who see it as a sedentary, polite, after-dinner recreation have not played the game as it is really played.

CROQUET is the first book published in the United States to cover all the aspects of croquet, and the first published anywhere to include the newly codified, official U.S.C.A. rules. The book is roughly divided into three sections. The first presents the history and lore of the sport, from its introduction, through its Hollywood days, to the present. The major part is devoted to the play of the game. All aspects are covered; from the court and equipment, to the more complex principles of strategy. You might find it helpful, especially if you are a beginning player, to bring the balls to the court and walk through a game, experimenting with the various shots, and testing the different strategies outlined in the book. The final part of *CROQUET* contains the official U.S. rules, an extensive glossary, records, and a list of clubs.

CROQUET contains everything that the croquet player, from beginner to expert, needs to know about America's fastest growing and most misunderstood sport.

—Andrew I. Adler, Roger Adler
Editors

*The ingenuity of man has never
conceived anything better calculated to
bring out all the evil passions of
humanity than the so-called game of
croquet... Our forefathers early
recognized the insidious wickedness of
the game and rooted it out.*
—*Living Age,* circa 1898

*Rutherford B. Hayes also liked to play
croquet on the White House lawn, but
even there the Democrats would not let
him alone. They charged he had
squandered six dollars of taxpayers
money for a set of fancy boxwood croquet
balls.*
—*The American Past*
Roger Butterfield, 1957

I
Croquet:
Lore and Legend

The origin of croquet, like that of many other sports, is obscure. Although the game has been played in roughly its present form for about one hundred years, its antecedents extend back many centuries. As long ago as the fourteenth century, peasants in Brittany and Southern France amused themselves playing a game called *Paille Maille,* in which crude mallets were used to knock balls through hoops made of bent willow branches. This ancestral version of croquet persisted, and by the seventeenth century, *Pele Mele,* as it was called in England, had become popular with Charles II and his court. Diarist Samuel Pepys, in his entry of April 2, 1661, wrote that "I went into St. James Parke, where I saw the Duke of Yorke playing at Pesle Mesle—the first time that I ever saw that sport." Pall Mall, as the game came finally to be called, was played with a curved club, a wooden ball, and two hoops. The court was often made of powdered cockleshells, and the hoops were decorated with flowers. The game lost favor in the 18th and 19th centuries, and little was heard of it until the 1850's.

In 1852 or 1853, croquet was introduced into England from Ireland, where a game called *crooky,* which used implements similar to the modern ones, had been played in Portarlington, Queen's County, Kilkee, in County Clare, and Kingstown, near Dublin, since the 1830's. No one knows how the game reached Ireland, although it has been suggested that it was introduced by French nuns or possibly by French refugees. According to the Oxford English Dictionary, the word "croquet" is a form of the word *croche,* an old North French word used to mean 'shepherd's crook'. The word is found in more modern French dialects, where it is used to mean 'hockey stock'. Although most agree that croquet's origin is French, it has been proposed by A.G. Ross that the game was actually born in Ireland. He claims that "croquet" came from the Irish word *cluiche,* which means 'play', and is pronounced roughly

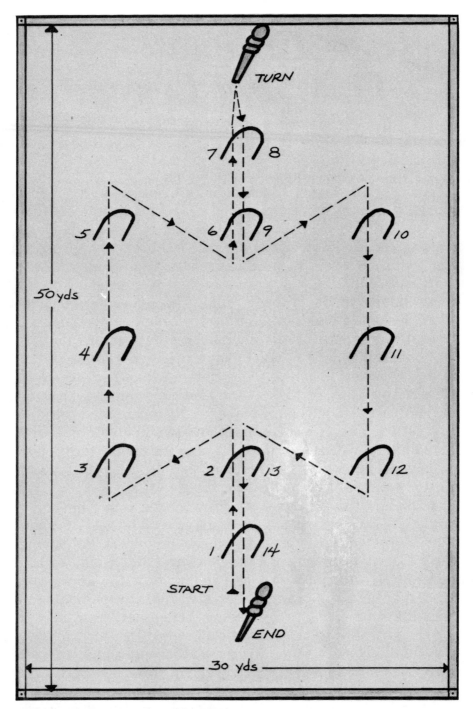

The standard court setting of the 1860's.
With six to eight wickets, this layout
provided little challenge for the serious
player.

like 'crooky'. According to Ross, the phrase "to take croquet" might be a translation of the Irish *gabail do cluiche,* which means, literally, to take to playing, or to begin to play.

Wherever its origins lie, croquet was introduced into England from Ireland in the early 1850's by one Mr. Spratt, who had been given a set of croquet implements by a Miss McNaughten around 1840. Miss McNaughten informed Mr. Spratt that the game had been introduced into Ireland but that she had seen it in its primitive state in either Southern France or Italy. The crude and rustic game observed by Miss McNaughten was played with hoops made of willow rods. The villagers constructed the mallets by boring a hole in a hard, knotty piece of wood and inserting a broomstick for the handle. Mr. Spratt kept the croquet equipment for several years before selling it to Mr. Jaques, an enterprising young man, whose family is the foremost manufacturer of croquet equipment today. It was Mr. Jaques who brought the game to notice. Incidentally, the unfortunate Miss McNaughten perished in a fire soon after giving the equipment to Mr. Spratt.

By 1865, croquet had achieved wide acceptance and had spread throughout England and its colonies. One gentleman of the time, noting in a letter to a friend that the game was introduced into India "during the hot weather of 1864 at Simla," observed that "the Viceroy played with an entire mallet of ivory—as became his position." During these early days of popularity in England, croquet was primarily an after-dinner recreation. It was played with ten large hoops, two pegs, and odd-sized mallets, on a lawn that measured 50 by 30 yards. The game was played as a sequence game, which meant that the turns *and* the balls were played sequentially according to the color of the ball. It is usually still played this way in the United States, though in Great Britain, in singles, while the turns alternate, the balls may be played in any order.

Croquet's great popularity in England continued through the 1860's and into the 1870's. In 1861, *Routledge's Handbook of Croquet* appeared. This book, probably the sport's first rule book, still basically governs the game. Another important and influential publication of the time was *Croquet: A Treatise and Commentary,* by Captain Mayne Reid, a hero of the Mexican War and the author of several books for boys. Captain Reid, whose book appeared in England in 1863 and in New York in 1869, saw croquet as a healthy, and presumably safer, substitute for war, and warned his readers of

Members of the family of British Prime Minister Gladstone playing croquet at Fasque, Kincardineshire in the 1860's.

the dangers of encountering women on the croquet court.

The 1860's also saw the appearance of the game's first recorded champions. In 1867 Walter Jones-Whitmore won a tournament at Evesham and became, according to some, croquet's first champion. Jones-Whitmore was also the first to attempt to devise a system of strategy and tactics, which he published in a book called *Croquet Tactics* in 1868. One year after Jones-Whitmore's victory at Evesham, Walter Peel, one of the major figures in the history of croquet, became the game's first true champion, and by 1869, the All-England Croquet Club was founded at Wimbledon. When Peel won his championship, the hoops were six inches wide, five inches wide for the final two rounds. In the game's early days the hoops had been as wide as eight inches, but they were gradually reduced in size to four inches by 1872. Early in the 1870's lawn tennis was introduced in England, and, for a while, the controversy over which was the best game, tennis or croquet, became quite intense. Soon, however, lawn tennis eclipsed croquet in popularity, and English croquet entered a period of decline that lasted through the 1880's.

Croquet was introduced to the United States in the early 1870's. The sport was first taken up by high society in the New York area, but it soon achieved general popularity throughout the country. Lawn tennis was introduced here at about the same time, but from the 1870's through the 1890's, croquet enthusiasts far outnumbered the tennis players. A croquet set was mandatory equipment for every estate, and civic leaders provided sets for public parks, which previously had not had facilities for any sport played on grass. Croquet was quite popular with women and was one of the first games played in the United States by both sexes. To this day, it is the only sport in which men and women compete with a similar handicap. Women players are more prominent today in Australia than in any other country (the current singles champion of that country is Mrs. V. Crane of Victoria). In 1882, the National Croquet Association was formed to help supervise the game. The association was active into the 1890's when lawn tennis suddenly surged in popularity, and croquet enthusiasm began to wane. The ebb in croquet's popularity was due, in part, to the game's surprisingly unsavory reputation. It had become associated with gambling, drinking, and philandering to such an extent that it was banned in Boston by one Reverend Skinner, and several articles of the time called upon both clergy and laity to suppress "the immoral practice of croquet."

It wasn't until the mid-1890's that interest in croquet began to revive in England, and several years later the sport's popularity began to return in the United States. Although croquet was played in a few places, tournaments had all but disappeared. The game was still played as a sequence game, with hoops whose dimensions had been reduced from four inches to three and one quarter inches in 1871. One year later, the Hale setting of six hoops and two pegs was introduced, and this setting continued in use for the next fifty years, although the hoop dimensions were again enlarged. The croquet renaissance began in 1896 when Walter Peel and Captain Drummond founded the United All-England Croquet Association at Roehampton, England. This organization, with typical British understatement, is called the Croquet Association and is still the ruling body of British and Commonwealth croquet. The final rounds of the All-England Handicap, one of croquet's most important championships, are played annually at Roehampton. Croquet's resurgence was aided by the arrival of Cyril Corbally, who, along with other great Irish players such as Duff Matthews and Leslie O'Callaghan, introduced new skills and tactics to the game. Croquet's popularity continued undiminished until the outbreak of World War I.

An ocean away, croquet's revival began in the United States. In 1899, a small group of players from the United States met in Norwich, Connecticut to revise the old Routledge Rules and revitalize the game. The new rules provided for standardized court size, reduced hoop dimensions, and the use of only four balls instead of the cumbersome eight. Two balls were used by each player, or two per team for doubles.

Croquet's popularity in the United States has been increasing since the end of World War I. In the 1930's the WPA and the National Recreation Association added croquet sets to their inventory of standard playground equipment. The sport also became a status favorite of literary and entertainment people in the '30's and '40's. East Coast players, such as George S. Kaufman, Alexander Woollcott, and Dorothy Parker, developed a fierce and unsportsman-like rivalry with West Coast players such as Harpo Marx, Darryl Zanuck, and George Sanders.

In 1922, the Willis setting of six hoops and one peg was

Harpo Marx and George S. Kaufman at their favorite pastime.

introduced in England. This layout is still the one most used today. During the mid-20's, the first test matches for the MacRobertson Shield, croquet's international trophy, were held when Australia sent a team to England in 1925. This trophy is still competed for every few years, with the next competition scheduled for 1979 in New Zealand. England, winner of the 1974 test matches held there, is the defending champion.

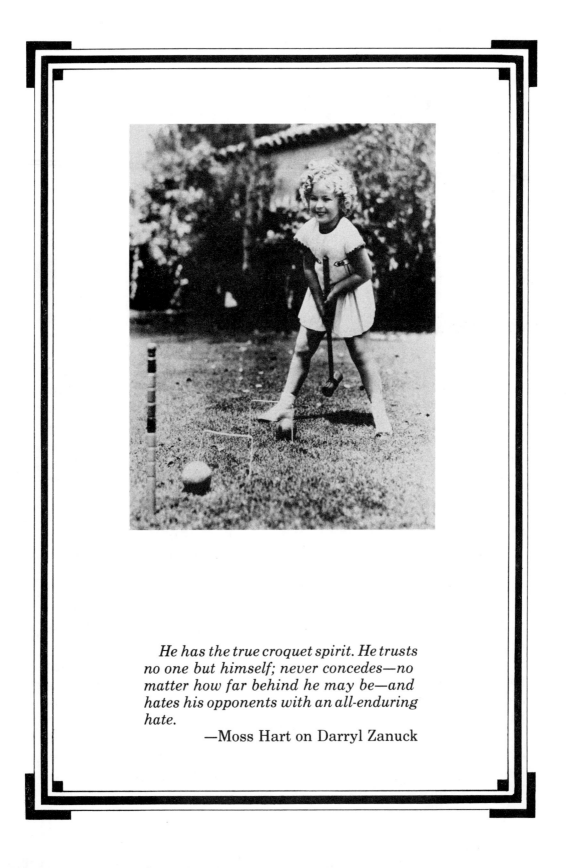

He has the true croquet spirit. He trusts no one but himself; never concedes—no matter how far behind he may be—and hates his opponents with an all-enduring hate.

—Moss Hart on Darryl Zanuck

II
Croquet Comes Back
to the U.S.A.

After the First World War, American croquet, like tennis, had become a fashionable pastime or, worse yet, a game to be played occasionally with the children in the back yard.

Then in the '20's croquet became popular again, mainly through the efforts—and competition—of two men; Alexander Woollcott—author, columnist and critic—and Herbert Bayard Swope, publisher of the *New York World* , Woollcott's friend, enemy and sometime employer. Woollcott had taken his croquet mallet with him when he went away to Hamilton college and had been playing for years before his arrival in New York. Swope brought the game and equipment back from England, and together he and Woollcott helped to introduce nine-wicket, two stake, no boundaries croquet to the New York theatre and literary crowd. Woollcott was a founding member of that legendary literary set, the Algonquin Roundtable, and was probably the most experienced, and certainly fiercest, competitor among those who played. Competition was eagerly provided by Moss Hart, George Kaufman, Neysa McNein, Franklin P. Adams, Charles MacArthur, and others. Kaufman, because he was slender and had a frenzied manner of gripping the mallet, was referred to by Woollcott as "a morning glory climbing a pole." Kaufman was also the target of another barb when Richard Rodgers allowed "that Kaufman was very good in the theatre but very bad on the croquet field." Kaufman was certainly never short of the appropriate quip himself, and once, when Heywoud Broun arrived for play decked out in a grass length coat that may have cost the lives of every raccoon in New York State, Kaufman cautioned him "not to bend over in Central Park."

One of the most avid players in the group was Harpo Marx, who later helped to popularize the sport on the West Coast. Harpo was so serious a player he had a spare bedroom converted into a storeroom for his croquet equipment. It was even air conditioned to keep the temperature constant and protect his purchases. Not stopping there, he talked a neighbor into letting him convert a flat-roofed garage into a practice croquet field. All told, Harpo estimated that the group spent $50,000 on equipment, a sizable sum considering the period and the fact that a comparatively small initial investment is usually all that's needed. As Kaufman recalled, "the only true winner of the game was the firm of Abercrombie and Fitch, which supplied English mallets, balls and wickets at prices just this side of keeping a string of polo ponies."

Harpo once interrupted a meeting that was going on between Alexander Woollcott and Eleanor Roosevelt by banging practice shots up and down the hallway outside Alex's apartment. Whether it was because of this or not, Woollcott eventually deserted New York for a retreat on Neshobe Island, located in the middle of Lake Bomoseen, Vermont, where he continued his writing and, of course, croquet playing. Weekend visitors were captive players for Woollcott, since he refused to allow them to return to the mainland until he had wrung a victory from them on the croquet court. As one guest put it, Woollcott "was impossible in victory, irascible in defeat." In one memorable match Harpo Marx needed only to hit, or roquet, Woollcott's ball to cinch the match, but there was a maple tree between the two balls. Harpo dragged out an old auto tire, sawed it in half, and put it around the tree, and came out the other side smacking Woollcott's ball. Furious, Alex stamped off, referring to Harpo as a "fawn's behind." Like the tale of Babe Ruth calling his home run, this story has also gotten a bit hazy with time. Another version has Harpo, confronted with the same situation, paying Woollcott's gardener $100 to dig a trench around the tree. In either case, the shot resulted in a perfect roquet.

Herbert Bayard Swope Sr., publisher of the *New York World*, was an aggressive competitor in everything he undertook, not the least of which was croquet. On his estate at Sands Point, Long Island, he built a course so large that players had to shout to one another. It was complete with sand traps, bunkers, a rough and was edged with a metal retaining rim to keep the grass from intruding onto the court. Once off the court, a player needed several shots to get back on, including a mild wedge shot to pop the ball over the rim. Once Swope ordered his partner, after a hit shot, to "destroy" the other ball by driving it off the court. When his partner started to protest, Swope roared: "Don't argue with me, dammit, do as I say."

Properly cowed, his partner followed instructions, and blasted the ball off the court and down the road leading to Long Island Sound. "Good work," said Swope, approvingly. Suddenly he did a double-take and screamed, "Good God, that was my ball!"

Swope was a true croquet maven, and Harpo recalls a match that he and Swope completed while then Governor of New York Al Smith was kept waiting on the telephone. Another time it became too dark to continue a match, but Swope had his quests ring the court with their cars and turn the lights on. The game was completed, but five cars had dead batteries as a result.

Another croquet aficionado is Averell Harriman. During a Thanksgiving party a snow storm came up while a game was in progress. Rather than stop the match, he hired eight men, complete with snow plows, shovels and a tractor, to clean the course. And the game went on. Harriman has had to make many sacrifices in the service of his country, but one thing he has not given up is his love of croquet. While ambassador to Russia, he demanded the Soviets set up a croquet course for his use. Later, serving as Secretary of Commerce, he was in San Francisco on business and called Darryl F. Zanuck to bemoan the fact that he hadn't been able to play croquet in a week. "Why you poor fellow," sympathized Zanuck, "fly down to Palm Springs." Harriman arrived at 11 p.m. and the two played on the lighted court till four in the morning. A tired but satisfied Harriman then boarded a plane for Washington. Zanuck, known in croquet circles as "The Terrible-tempered Mr. Bang" for his aggressive style of play, was probably the main reason croquet became popular in Hollywood after the Second World War. As Moss Hart said, "Zanuck has the true croquet spirit. He trusts no one but himself; never concedes—no matter how far behind he may be—and he hates his opponents with an all-enduring hate."

Zanuck had constructed a magnificent 80′ by 82′ croquet court in Hollywood that was complete with a water hazard. Upkeep alone in those pre-inflation days was $14,000 a year, and stakes on some of the matches were reported to be as high as $10,000 a game. Among the notables who played there were Tyrone Power, Howard Hawkes, Mike Romanoff, George Sanders and Louis Jourdan. Another regular was Gregory Ratoff, the Russian actor and impresario, who was so fat he played with the mallet held under his arm.

Louis Jourdan was by far the best player, due in part to his exposure to the subtleties of the British game. It was not

Darryl F. Zanuck's home croquet course.

unusual for him to go around the course in one turn, and he was said to be accurate on shots up to 100 feet. When Sam Goldwyn built two courses in Beverly Hills, George Sanders suggested sand traps for the main court to stop Jourdan but "it only slowed him up about ten minutes." Today Jourdan is still a first class player but, as one wag commented, "Louis never really gained his confidence on the croquet court until after making GIGI."

Another Hollywood player is actor Gig Young who, during one match, was faced with a very difficult shot. The court, situated near the San Andreas fault, was shaken by a tremor that caused everyone to run for cover. Upon returning to the court, it was discovered that Young's ball was now in a perfect position to run the hoop. Gig smiled and commented wryly "it must have been an act of God."

Although there was a great deal of croquet interest in Hollywood during the 40's, the Eastern players still considered themselves the best. To settle the issue, the first and only East-West championship was held in 1946. Over 300 Hollywood names, including Clifton Webb, Douglas Fairbanks and Howard Hughes, showed up at Hawkes' ranch in Palm Springs for the crucial match.

The East squad of Tyrone Power and agent Fefe Ferry was led by Moss Hart, while the West was represented by Zanuck—as captain, of course—and Howard Hawkes. Hart was more careful in this match than he had been the previous summer when he had attempted to whack an opponent's ball into the next county and hit his foot instead, spending six weeks on crutches.

Alexander Woollcott: "Irascible in victory, impossible in defeat."

The West won the first match but, even with Zanuck protesting every shot, the East came back to win the second game and set up the all-important rubber game. By the time the third match was to be played it was evening, and the lights had to be turned on. One critical play occurred during the game when Tyrone Power had to drive Zanuck's ball as far as possible. Hart sidled up and whispered, "Remember *'Daytime Wife,'* a turkey produced by Zanuck starring Power. Properly aroused, Tyrone sent the ball winging. A turning point occurred when Zanuck flubbed a shot early in the match and someone in the crowd yelled, "Well, that's one shot he can't retake." Zanuck never did identify the culprit, but his game was off and the East went on to win the third match.

The three games lasted a total of 11 hours and, toward the end, things did get a bit loose. As Hart put it, "Cheating is as much a part of croquet as it is of poker, but in the dark it got out of control." Nonetheless, the winning East team complained bitterly about the size of the victor's cup, which was hardly visible to the naked eye.

Although Zanuck is a serious croquet player, some frivolity does creep into his game. When someone new was introduced to the game at his place in Palm Springs, they were given "the ball" to use. This was a ball that looked like any other ball but was canted to roll every way but straight. Mike Romanoff, a good and good-natured croquet player, was the butt of several of Zanuck's practical jokes. "We gave Romanoff a ball once that was painted just like a grapefruit. Then he hit it under a tree with a lot of real grapefruits lying around. He went around there for twenty minutes whacking the hell out of real grapefruit. He was absolutely drenched with grapefruit juice."

Zanuck has another favorite Romanoff story as well. "Then there's 'the mallet'. It's my personal mallet I tell Romanoff, and I want him to have it because it's so delicately balanced it will make a crack player out of him—finest wood from the Himalayas and absolutely without price. Only, for God's sake, under no circumstances is he to lay it down or throw it away.

"Well, of course, it's a breakaway mallet and along about the third swing the thing falls into splinters. Of course, the boob is white-faced and I'm having a stroke. I fall to the ground and wail, 'it's irreplaceable, the mallet's irreplaceable'."

In the late fifties and until his death, one of the most hallowed croquet grounds in America were the two courts at Sam Goldwyn's Beverly Hills estate. Along with the other Hollywood regulars mentioned above Goldwyn would play for hours on end with visiting East Coast aficionados such as TV Producer William O. Harback, Nick Vanoff and authors Peter Maas and George Plimpton. Mrs. Goldwyn was finally compelled to abolish play on the courts just before Sam's death because he would get overly excited in his bedroom listening to the sound of mallets hitting balls while friends were playing below the window.

Meanwhile, in the East, croquet was entering a new and vigorous era. Centering in the Long Island South Shore resort communities of Westhampton Beach and Southampton, two separate groups independently began to form what has become the nucleus of the resurgence and popularity of the game today.

By 1966, the Americans had progressed far enough to send a three man team consisting of Homer Landon, Henri White, and Walter Margulies against the Hurlingham Croquet Club in England, an example of enthusiasm triumphing over experience. Hurlingham, which has seven croquet courts, has over 1000 members and is to croquet what Wimbledon (once known as the Wimbledon Croquet and Tennis Club) is to tennis. The American squad was soundly thrashed in its first venture into international competition, but the players learned many valuable tips and points of strategy. As one Londoner remarked airily, "You Americans play a primitive croquet, the kind we used to play 50 years ago."

Undaunted, the Americans issued a challenge the following year, and this time the British team journeyed to New York to play at the Westhampton Mallet Club. This time the match was played under American nine-wicket rules, and the games ended in a three-to-three tie.

The series went back to Hurlingham in 1968, and, playing under British rules, the Americans were soundly defeated 8 to 0.

Croquet courts based on the English layout (not all, but many of putting green quality) have been put down in Long Island, New York, Palm Beach, Bermuda and California. Clubs from these areas have painstakingly (and sometimes painfully) adapted, modified, and amended local rule variations into the American six-wicket croquet game. These clubs, as the founding members of The United States Croquet Association, have adopted them for their own and inter-club tournament play. During this period, more and more Americans and their neighbors in Bermuda and Jamaica have taken up the game in earnest, with top players reaching levels of skill formidable enough to challenge our English friends on their own grounds as well as here in the U.S.

Although American six-wicket rules do now and will probably continue to differ from the Laws of the British Association, the U.S.C.A. is confident that Americans practicing the British style will expand their shot-making skills and their ultimate enjoyment of croquet.

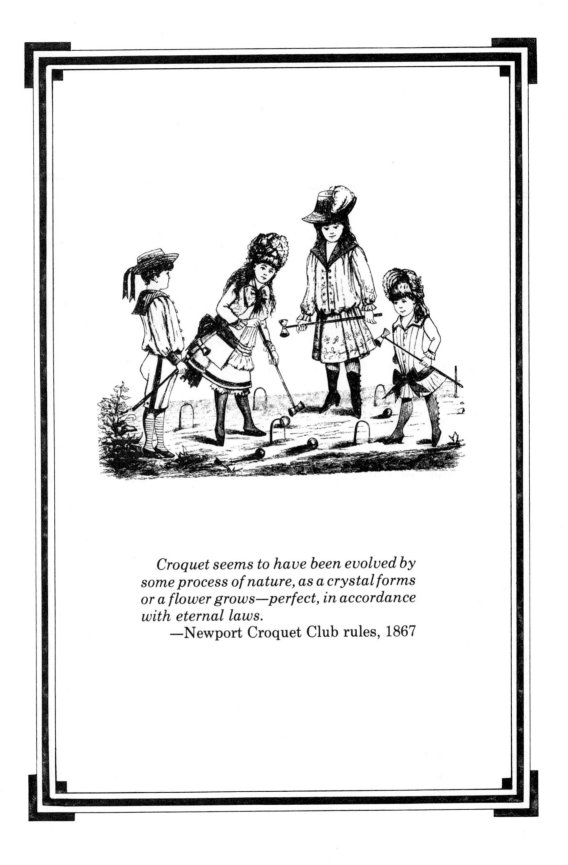

Croquet seems to have been evolved by
some process of nature, as a crystal forms
or a flower grows—perfect, in accordance
with eternal laws.
    —Newport Croquet Club rules, 1867

III
Beginning Play

We have all seen croquet players—sedentary types who apparently take turns tapping a ball around a lawn. That's croquet—a simple, literally childish game. It is certainly not a sport and hardly the mental challenge of an evenly matched chess game, to say nothing of the physical challenge of a strong set of tennis. Croquet, one of the oldest forms of team play, is, in fact, a gruelling game, an uncompromising sport, demanding control, skill, intelligence and stamina.

Croquet is probably America's most misunderstood sport. Mention croquet and most people think of the back yard game with short-handled mallets, and nine thin wire wickets placed in a "double diamond" set-up with a wooden stake at each end. Serious croquet is quite a different thing; rather like comparing softball with the kids to the L.A. Dodgers.

To start with, the equipment used in competitive croquet is much more business-like; heftier mallets, larger balls and, in place of the thin wire hoops, heavy, rather formidable steel wickets; with a clearance one-eighth of an inch wider than the balls. And in place of the familiar nine-wicket layout we all grew up with, there is the more challenging six-wicket layout with one lone stake in the middle. This six-wicket layout is used in all international competition and in all U.S. Croquet Association (USCA) tournaments, while the nine-wicket "bust 'em into the next county" game has been relegated to the back yard.

Most of the points discussed in the following chapters can be applied to both the nine-wicket and six-wicket games. Running a wicket or executing a split shot is the same whatever the game and you will find as you read through the rules, there are fewer differences between the two than might be thought. So when we talk about croquet in this book we are referring to the standard six wicket game and, unless noted, not the nine-wicket version. Make sure you understand the chapter on principals and the chapter on

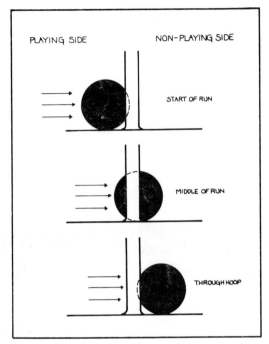

When a ball is through a wicket.

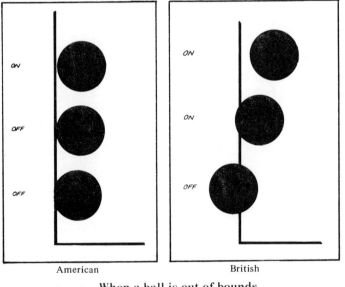

American   British

When a ball is out of bounds.

the court layout; this will give you general background before forging ahead to the challenge of croquet.

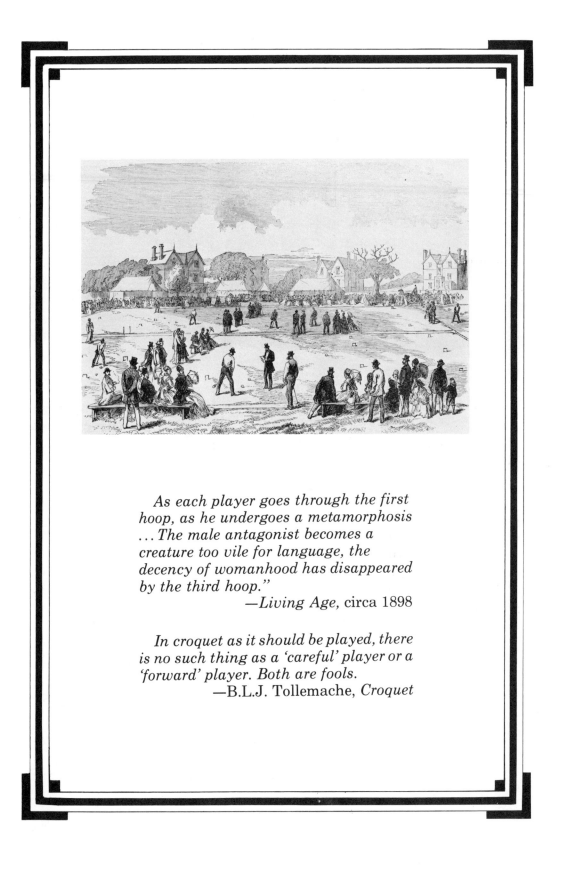

*As each player goes through the first
hoop, as he undergoes a metamorphosis
... The male antagonist becomes a
creature too vile for language, the
decency of womanhood has disappeared
by the third hoop."*
                    —*Living Age*, circa 1898

*In croquet as it should be played, there
is no such thing as a 'careful' player or a
'forward' player. Both are fools.*
                    —B.L.J. Tollemache, *Croquet*

IV
Basic Principles of Play

American croquet, unlike the British version, is a sequence game, i.e. the blue, red, black and yellow balls are hit in successive turns. The British game is non-sequence; a player could elect to hit the blue ball (assuming, in singles, he is playing blue and black) on several successive turns. The object of the game is to score more points than your opponent, by hitting your two balls through a course of six wickets twice and, finally, against a center peg. Each ball must run each wicket in the proper sequence and from the appropriate direction. The winner is the player(s) who makes a circuit of the course first with both balls or, in a time-limit game, the side with the greatest number of points when time is called.

The proper direction of play is as follows: first go through the four outside hoops, then hoops five and six in the center. These wickets are then scored in the opposite direction; the second wicket becomes 1-back (the seventh wicket you must run), the first wicket becomes 2-back and so on.

Each wicket, or hoop-stop, made in the proper order by each ball is worth one point, as is the peg, for a total of 13 points. Thus, a side of one or two players can score a maximum of 26 points. In the U.K. and Australia the full scores are usually given (e.g. 26-14, 26-9), although sometimes the difference between the game scores of the players is given (a shutout is recorded as + or − 26). In the United States, however, only the winners and losers are noted, not their scores.

Croquet is a game of alternating turns. In doubles matches, the ball assigned on the first stroke must be the one used throughout the match. In singles matches, the striker alternates balls but the ball that a player starts with on a particular turn must be played for the duration of the turn.

Play is made in croquet by hitting a ball with a mallet. The person doing this is called the striker. A turn is one stroke, but extra strokes may be earned in two ways. One way is by running a hoop in the proper order. This earns one "continuation" stroke. The second method is by making a roquet—hitting another ball with your own. This entitles you to a "croquet" shot and a continuation shot. While this is the general rule, you should note the following exceptions: First, once you have roqueted a ball, you are said to be 'dead' on that ball, and cannot hit it again until you have gone through your next wicket. Second, if a wicket is run during a croquet shot, the extra continuation stroke is forfeited. A player can never earn more than one croquet and one continuation stroke on any one shot. Third, hoop strokes are not cumulative. If you run two wickets, or hoops, on the same stroke—possible, but exceptionally rare—you still earn only one continuation stroke. If you run all the wickets in a single turn you have achieved an "all-round break", croquet's equivalent of a no-hitter.

At the game's opening each side chooses for the starting order by flipping a coin. One side takes the red and yellow balls, the other blue and black. To start the game, the first striker plays the blue ball onto the course from a point a mallet's length in back of the first wicket. When the starting player's turn ends, his opponent, playing the red ball, begins, and the sequence continues until all four balls are entered into play. All balls are dead on each other until they have made the first wicket, so no real strategy occurs until the first hoop has been run. If all players but one make the first hoop, they are still dead on that player's ball until he has successfully run the hoop. This is true in singles as well as doubles.

In regulation croquet, when a ball is sent out of bounds, it is replaced at the sideline, a mallet's head in from where it left the course. If you ricochet your own ball off the course on a roquet shot there is no penalty. Your ball is replaced at the proper spot, and your continuation shot follows. You may not, however, knock a roqueted ball over the line without ending your turn. If you do hit another ball over the line (on a roquet or croquet shot), the balls are replaced one mallet head in from where they went out.

No further discussion of balls out of bounds can be made without explaining the situation known as "being in hand." This refers to balls that have to be lifted and repositioned during a turn. This arises when a ball lies on the boundary line, within a mallet's head of the line, or has gone over the line. The striker's ball is in hand only at the conclusion of his turn. If two or more balls have to be replaced, the opponent determines the order of their repositioning.

Although it has been explained in passing, it should be emphasized that being dead on one or more balls drastically affects play and strategy. You cannot hit a ball you are dead on until you have 'cleaned' yourself by clearing the next wicket. The penalty for hitting a dead ball is ending your turn, and the return of the balls to their original position. It is crucial not to become dead on multiple balls unless you are reasonably sure of running a wicket on your continuation shot. Being dead on several balls obviously limits your break and roquet-making abilities, and, hence, the duration of your turn. You should therefore plan ahead, weigh the potential gain or loss of each shot, and try to assure yourself the free use of all the balls. If you commit the error of becoming dead on two or three balls you can be sure your opponent will try to keep you in that position for as long as possible. Whenever you are in position to run your proper wicket and clean yourself of any deadness, your opponent will attempt to knock you away. As Darryl Zanuck put it, "when you're three ball dead, you're just a useless bum."

Conversely, it is to your advantage to keep your opponent from cleaning himself of any deadness. In some instances, when your opponent is "live" on your ball you might tempt him into hitting it, thereby making him dead on that ball.

It is imperative, in quality play at any level, to be aware of the status of each ball in the match. You should know which ball is the most advanced, which balls are alive, which are dead for each player, and which wickets each player is going for. Be especially aware of the playing order of each ball. Before sending a ball to a spot, review which ball will be shot next.

You will find that the tactics you adopt are determined by a variety of factors: the situation in hand, the quality of your opponent's play, your own abilities, the state of the game, and the court conditions. As you become more experienced, you will find that your tactics change from game to game as these variables change.

Generally speaking, it is best to play in a manner somewhere between angelic caution and foolish aggression. You should play it safe, if necessary, to prevent yourself from getting into an unfavorable position. Do not, however, in easing your own position, set your opponent up for a potentially damaging shot. Defensive play is also a big factor; cases will arise when you can block your foe's progress by strategic placement of your own balls.

These are just some of the basic principles of the game, and a few of the beginning strategies and tactics. Other points, as well as some of the more advanced techniques, will be touched upon in later chapters. But this review should give you an idea of some of the complexities involved in croquet as it is seriously played. It is a very different game as played under the rules of the United States Croquet Association, from the brand of croquet found in most back yards. Adopting some or all of the rules and recommendations in this book should greatly enhance the pleasure you get from the sport.

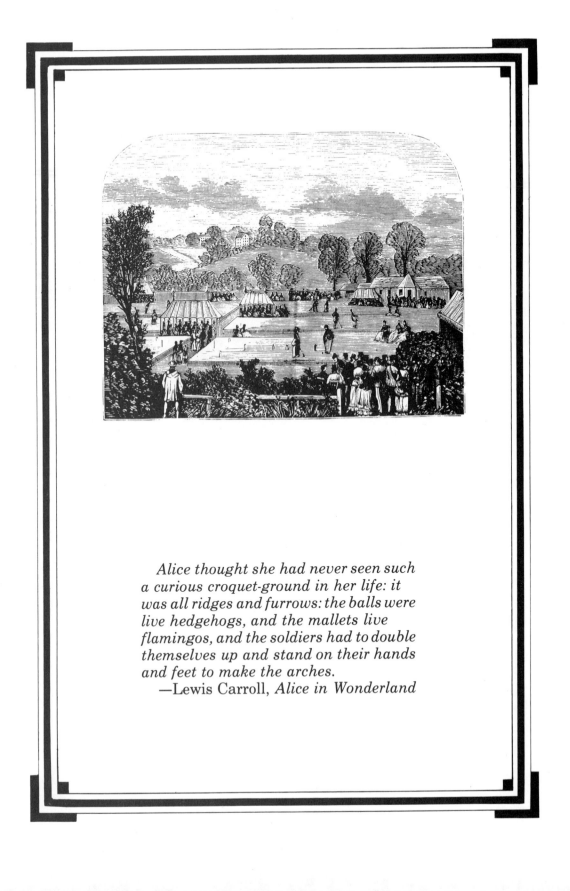

Alice thought she had never seen such a curious croquet-ground in her life: it was all ridges and furrows: the balls were live hedgehogs, and the mallets live flamingos, and the soldiers had to double themselves up and stand on their hands and feet to make the arches.
—Lewis Carroll, *Alice in Wonderland*

V
Court and Equipment

The standard American six-wicket croquet court, that used for tournament play, is a rectangle measuring 105 by 84 feet. If available space is too small for a full sized court, a proportionately smaller rectangle can be used, so long as the ratio of the sides is five to four. The boundaries of the court should be clearly marked. The inside edge of the border is the actual boundary line. The four corners of the court are known respectively as corners 1,2,3, and 4, and the boundaries are designated South, West, North and East, regardless of the geographical orientation of the court. Within this rectangle, the six wickets and one stake are laid out, with the stake placed at the intersection of the two diagonals. The corner wickets, known as the outer hoops, are set with their centers 21 feet from their adjacent boundaries. The center wickets, or inner hoops, are placed 21 feet from the stake. Of course, if your court is smaller than the standard size, the wickets should be arranged proportionately. Local conditions may require other layouts, but 50 x 40 feet is generally considered the minimum size for croquet.

Many players in the United States, especially backyard players, use a layout of nine wickets and two stakes, with one stake used as a starting and finishing peg, and the wickets laid out in a double diamond. Since there are few regulation courts in America, and since the game is often played in back yards and other available space, the size of the courts often varies considerably. Preferably, the court is placed on a flat, closely-cropped lawn, with the length twice the width, but many players incorporate hills, trees, streams, and other natural and man-made hazards into their courses.

The dimensions of the British standard court are the same as the American. There is, however, an unmarked inner rectangle one yard inside the court called the yard line. On each of the short sides of the yard line are other unmarked lines called baulk lines. The one on the bottom or south yard line extends from the west corner to the center of the yard line, and the one on the north side goes from the

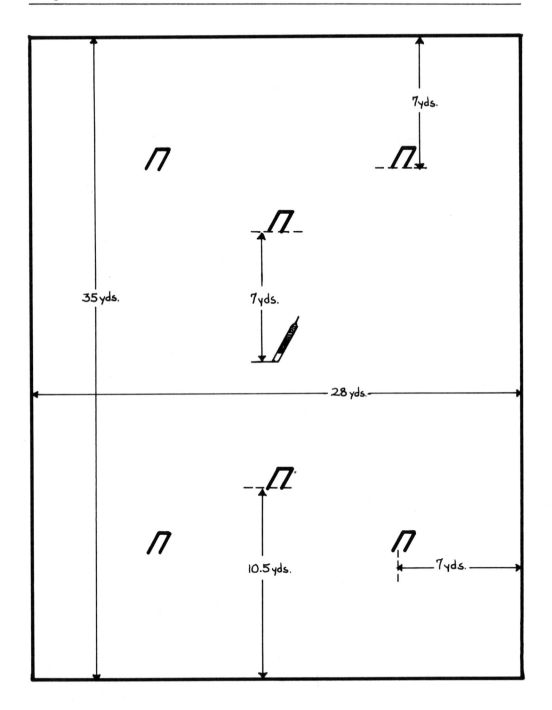

**Official United States Croquet
Association 6-wicket layout.**

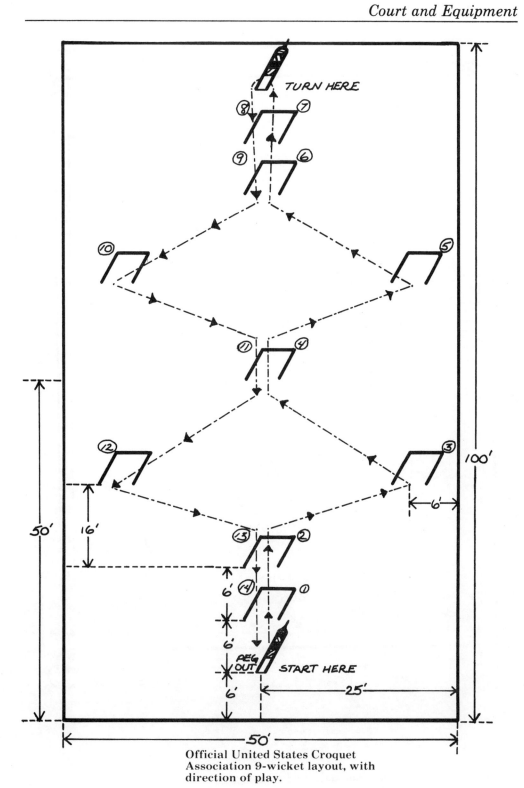

**Official United States Croquet
Association 9-wicket layout, with
direction of play.**

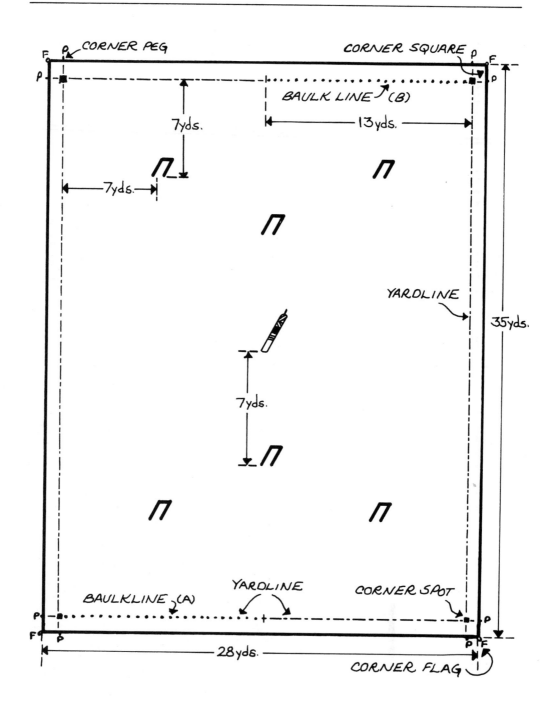

Standard British 6-wicket layout.

center of the yard line to the east corner. All the hoops are placed parallel to the north and south boundaries. In the American game, the rover wicket is played pointing inwards to the stake, the major difference between the two settings.

Equipment

"There are really two great moments for a croquet player, aside from winning a game. The first is when he is introduced to croquet. The second is when he feels he is good enough to order his own mallet with his initials on top of the handle."
—Peter Maas

Mallets, wickets, and balls, along with stakes and a few accessories used for guidance and keeping track of the play, comprise the basic equipment necessary to play croquet. The mallet is the most important piece of equipment and will be discussed last. Most casual players in this country have used the rounded, flexible wire hoops that come with most garden sets. The official wickets are quite different. They are made of rounded iron 5/8 of an inch in diameter and are of uniform thickness. They are solid and not at all

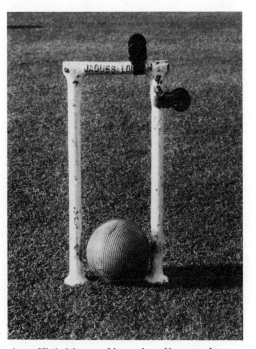

An official hoop. Note the clips used to mark the progress of each ball.

45

A standard wicket, with, at right, a
winter wicket. Note the thinner
uprights of the winter hoop.

flexible. There should be a foot clearance between the top of the
crown of the wicket and the ground. The crown is straight and at
right angles to the uprights. The distance between the uprights
must not be less than 3 11/16th inches or more than four inches.
The distance between the uprights should be uniform for the entire
wicket. All the wickets are painted white, but the crown of the first
wicket is painted blue, that of the last or "rover" painted red. The
wickets, of course, should be firmly fixed in the ground. There is
another, lighter form of wicket usually referred to as winter wickets,
because they are more easily placed in the hard, frozen ground.
They are 7/16ths of an inch in diameter, with the same clearance as
regular hoops. They are used in non-tournament games as the
conditions warrant.

The stake is made of wood and is 18 inches above the ground. It
is painted white, with blue, red, black, and yellow bands descending

in that order from the top. The stake must be vertical and firmly planted in the ground. Some stakes have an extension attached to the top to hold the clips. There are four clips, one the color of each ball, and they are used in play to designate to the players the progress of the respective balls. They are placed on the crown of the next hoop in sequence for the initial six wickets, and on the upright of each wicket for the return six. They are attached to the stake extension when a player is going for the peg.

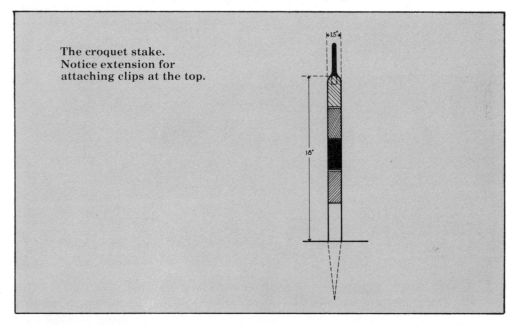

The croquet stake.
Notice extension for
attaching clips at the top.

The four croquet balls are colored, respectively, blue, red, black, and yellow, and are usually made of wood or composite. Other materials may be used as long as they are consistent. All the balls must weigh the same, and their weight must be between 15 3/4 ounces and 16 1/4 ounces. Their diameter must be 3 5/8 inches. This leaves a clearance between ball and wicket of between 1/16 and 3/8 of an inch. This, obviously, is very small indeed, and makes accuracy extremely important. Corner pegs and corner flags, which serve to delineate the corner squares, make up the rest of the court equipment.

Mallets
The mallet is the only piece of croquet equipment that the player can choose to his liking. Since you do have a choice, it is best

to take your time, look around, and try a few before you pick. There is a large range of equipment available in all price ranges and qualities, from inexpensive garden sets to custom made mallets costing hundreds of dollars. Serious players have for years ordered theirs made by John Jacques of Surrey, England. Jaques equipment is available in a number of stores in metropolitan areas of the United States.

Placing a clip, in the 19th century. At the height of croquet's popularity, candle sockets were attached to the wicket for night play.

A deadness board. Note that blue is 3-ball dead.

There are no weight or size restrictions on mallets. Years ago, the tendency was toward the heavier mallet, but today most weigh around three pounds, with three pounds, nine ounces considered heavy. The shaft of the mallet is usually about three feet long, and the shorter Irish style mallets about two feet eight inches long. As a general rule, a shorter shaft gives a player greater freedom of movement, while a longer one provides greater steadiness. The shaft is most commonly made of ash, although hickory and Malacca cane are also used. Cane shafts are the springiest, and hickory, although more subject to warpage than the others, probably provides the best combination of strength and spring. The grip area on the shaft is frequently bound with cork, string, or even a golf grip. Non-slipping suede can also be used. Most mallets have octagonal grips, but oval grips are also used.

The head of the mallet must be wood, but metal may be used for weighting or strengthening. Lignum vitae and boxwood are the most common mallet-head materials. Lignum vitae tends to be brittle, so heads of this wood should be brass bound. The heads may be round, or square and flat-bottomed. Both styles are popular in the United States. The square type is most popular in Australia and New Zealand, while the cylindrical style is favored in Britain. All work equally well, so the choice is largely a matter of personal taste.

The balancing point of the mallet should be about 1/5 of the distance from the bottom of the head to the top of the shaft. It is a good idea not to buy any extra shaft that isn't handled. Shorter shafts may be ordered, or you can cut it down from the top, but be *very* careful or the balance of the mallet will be destroyed. Make sure that the shaft is straight and the hole in the head for the shaft is accurately bored. The Rev. Elvey, a former president of the British Croquet Council, suggests that it is good to have the grain of the shaft at a 90° angle to the head or exactly parallel to the head. This can offset warpage. If your mallet gets wet, always dry it off before you store it. You can use varnish or shellac for weatherproofing. When your mallet is not in use, hang it upside down between two pegs. Don't store it in a corner, as this will put the handle out of proper alignment. And *never* use your mallet for any purpose other than its proper one. With decent care, a quality mallet can last a lifetime.

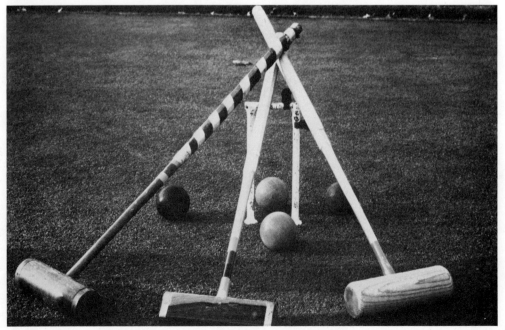

A round-headed and a square-headed mallet.

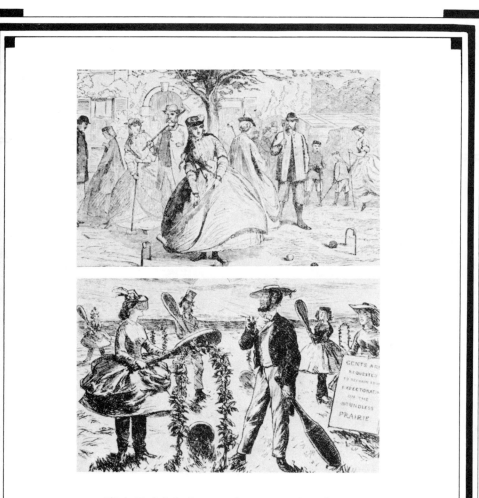

The British form of croquet is a better game than ours...more sportsman-like. Ours is a more strategic game and far more emotional. In our game you do what you call 'destroying' your opponent. The British don't go so far. They wouldn't think of doing things like some of our former leaders, like the late Alexander Woollcott. Why, he had his court beside a lake and thought nothing of knocking a guest's ball in the water. That sometimes caused trouble.

—Averell Harriman

VI
American vs. British Rules and Styles of Play

British croquet is as different from American croquet as cricket is from baseball. Like many American customs, croquet rules in the United States were originally based on the game played by our British cousins, but as the English game evolved, Yankee ingenuity (or an historic disregard for the way it's done elsewhere) refused to adapt to this evolution and brought about subtle and not so subtle changes in American croquet rules. Perhaps the American temperament is less to blame than the fact that as house lots became smaller in our growing land, the luxury of a regulation British court (eighty four by one hundred five feet of flat rolled lawn) restricted play to club grounds. Buffs who wished to play or practice on available greens began to improvise, and the inevitable changes or lack of changes were under way.

Croquet games in this country have tended to vary from lawn to lawn, depending essentially on good sportsmanship, force of personality and who owns the lawn. The movie mogul Sam Goldwyn is less known in croquet circles for his often quoted malaprops than for the fact that he installed a sandtrap on his court expressly to thwart the better-playing Louis Jourdan. This rather extreme example of rule flexibility proves the point made by English purists—American variations of the game have diluted it.

Aside from the visual similarity of the court setting there are quite a number of basic differences between croquet as played in Great Britain and either the American six-wicket or nine-wicket versions.

Clearly the most influential of these rules concerns "deadness". In the American game if you acquire "deadness" on any or all balls, you remain dead on them until you have cleared your next wicket. The British game provides that all "deadness" is cleared at the beginning of that ball's next turn, regardless of whether or not it has cleared its hoop.

The net effect of this difference is the greater emotional strain and thus more conservative nature of the American player facing the almost terminal condition of being "three ball dead" throughout the game. His English cousin may feel free to attempt more venturesome shots (and with this practice become more skillful at them) with less pressure or traumatic concern since he will be "alive" one way or another during his next turn.

Major layout changes are the invisible "yard line" set inside all boundary lines and two Baulk lines running one half the width of the South (from #1 corner) and North (from #3 corner) boundary lines in the English game. The Baulk areas are used to begin the game from any part thereof and to play legally lifted balls in hand from (after being wired or shot in during an English Advanced game).

In the American layout the yard line is reduced to a mallet-head (9″) and there are no baulk lines designated or used.

Other rules that tend to provide the English with the advantage of a looser, more wide-open game than the American versions are:

Rotation

(English:) Non-rotation play of either ball on a side during that sides turn. (Can decide pace of each ball's advance.)

(American:) Must play in rotation or sequence. (Causes better player to have to advance faster than weaker partner.)

Roquet
(out of bounds)

(English:) May roquet or rush a ball out-of-bounds and continue to play it.

(American:) Turn ends. (Ball usually ends up next to another ball which, if an opponent's ball, gives advantage to him.)

Rover

(English:) Only a rover may stake out another rover (Encourages bolder and faster play).

(American:) Any ball can put out a Rover (Penalizes leading ball) so slows progress.

Out of Bounds

(English:) Ball out of bounds is replaced one yard in bounds.

British direction of play.

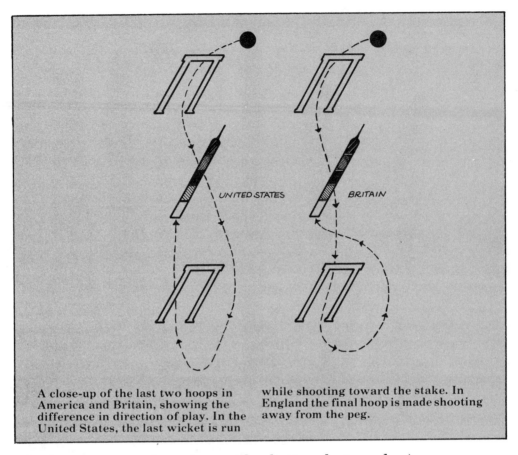

A close-up of the last two hoops in America and Britain, showing the difference in direction of play. In the United States, the last wicket is run while shooting toward the stake. In England the final hoop is made shooting away from the peg.

(Easier to approach and provides better shot angles.)
(American:)   One mallet-head in.

Bisques
(English:)   An English bisque is an additional shot from where the ball ends *after* a stroke.
(American:)   An American bisque shot is an additional shot from where the ball started before the stroke.

Lifts
(English:)   Allowed to lift a wired ball unable to hit any other ball and shoot from either baulk line.
(American:)   Not allowed.

Other differences which conversely provide somewhat more difficult moments for the English are:

Contact
(on croquet stroke)

(English:) Must make contact with roqueted ball in croquet stroke and move or shake that ball. (Difficult but effective shot.)

(American:) May take croquet stroke from up to mallet-head away. (Easier shot, less risk.)

Footing

(English: No foot shot allowed. (Forces more difficult split or croquet stroke.)

(American:) Footing allowed. (More effective than stop shot for sending croqueted ball long distances.)

Rover Wicket

(English:) Rover Hoop must be run going away from stake.

(American:) Rover wicket run inward toward stake. (Easier to stake out or clean deadness on ball for rover from this direction.)

Opening
(start of game)

(English:) Opening strokes of game are taken from either Baulk line (never stroked directly to No. 1 wicket) and balls are "alive" on all others after first stroke.

(American:) Begin game from one yard in front of wicket No. 1. (Balls are not alive until clearing No. 1 wicket.)

Summary: (U.S. vs. British)

The American six-wicket game is a more conservative, but nonetheless as interesting and challenging a game as the English. It places a greater premium on the strategically complex aspects of remembering deadness, rotation sequences, and assessing the strengths and weaknesses of the opponents than the British game.

The British, capitalizing on their less constricting rules, have thus been able to emphasize, and practice under game conditions, their shot-making skills. That is not to imply that the English game requires less strategy, but rather that it is a strategy more concerned with employing shooting strengths than the more conservative strategy of the Americans.

The chief difficulty Alice found at first was managing her flamingo: she succeeded in getting its body tucked away, comfortable enough, under her arm, with its legs hanging down, but generally, just as she had got its neck nicely straightened out, and was going to give the hedgehog a blow with its head, it would twist itself around and look up at her, with such a puzzled expression that she could not help bursting out laughing; and, when she had got its head down, and was going to begin again, it was very provoking to find that the hedgehog had unrolled itself, and was in the act of crawling away: besides all this, there was generally a furrow or ridge in the way wherever she wanted to send the hedgehog to, and, as the double up soldiers were always getting up and walking off to other parts of the ground, Alice came to the conclusion that it was a very difficult game indeed.

—Lewis Carroll, *Alice In Wonderland*

VII
Grips, Stances and the Swing

The Grip

There are essentially two ways to grip the croquet mallet. The most widely used method is called the reverse palm grip. With this grip, the palm of the upper hand faces the body, and that of the lower hand faces away from the body. The other widely used grip is called the Irish grip, which originated with the great Irish players at the turn of the century, such as Duff Matthews and Cyril Corbally. This grip has both palms facing away from the body. There are some variations of these two basic grips with interlocking or overlocking fingers. Most American players tend to separate their hands and move the lower hand down the shaft toward the head of the mallet. This is called the American style, and it is probably used because of the generally more rugged terrain of American courts, which require more leverage in the stroke than the smoother-surfaced English courts. British players usually keep their hands together close to the top of the mallet shaft, although many players, both British and American, employ both styles in the course of a game.

Comfort and success are the major factors in deciding which grip to use. The most important thing to remember is to have both hands working in concert, with neither hand gaining the mastery over the other. The type of shot you are attempting will also influence your choice of grip.

The Stance

There are three basic playing stances in croquet. In the oldest style, the golf style, you stand sideways to the object ball (the ball you are going to hit) and swing your mallet across your body like a golf club. Although you have good control with this stance, most of this advantage is lost by the added difficulty in aiming. As a result, this style is rarely used in tournament play today, though there are still a few good players, H.O. Hicks among them, who employ it quite effectively. The golf style is often used in garden croquet,

The reverse-palm grip. Also known as the conventional British grip.

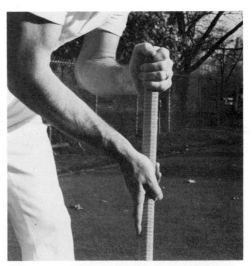

The spread reverse-palm grip. Also known as the conventional American upper grip.

The Irish grip.

Variation of reverse-palm grip.

because of the heavier grass. Because of its similarity to a golf swing, and the shorter mallet used, many Americans find it comfortable and easy to learn.

The two stances most widely used today are the front style and the center style. In the front style, which is also known as the upright style, you face the object ball and swing the mallet outside your feet. This stance allows for more freedom of movement and power than other stances, but it is more difficult to master. It also has the disadvantage that you are not hitting from directly behind the ball. You must guard against the tendency to swing around your body rather than directly towards the ball. You must take care to see that one hand does not predominate over the other. The front style requires a longer mallet than the center style, but it is less tiring.

In the center stance, you swing the mallet in pendulum-fashion between the legs. The advantage of this stance is that you stand behind the ball and swing directly in the line of aim. You must be careful in this stance to see that neither foot predominates. If that does happen, it can cause shots to miss to one side. The center style also requires more wrist control than the other stances.

The golf style.

The side style.

The Irish style is a variation of the center stance. The stance is basically the center stance with a shorter mallet and the Irish grip. The fingers should either overlock or interlock. Some players, 1974 and 1975 British Open Champion Nigel Aspinall among them, feel that the Irish style gives an advantage for longer shots. All are agreed that it is the most physically demanding of the playing styles.

59

The side style, from the side.

Front view of the center stance, with uneven weight distribution.

The center stance, with even weight distribution.

The center stance, with uneven weight distribution.

Standing too far from the ball will cause you to swing up at contact.

Standing too close to the ball will cause you to swing down at contact.

The Swing

One of the most difficult things to learn in the game of croquet is to hit the ball in the correct way. The first thing you must do before hitting the ball is to make sure your shot is lined up properly. In order to do this, you should walk up from behind the ball in the direction you wish to send it. This is called "stalking" the ball. Remember that the aim of the ball is determined not by the mallet but by the relation of your shoulders to the object ball. Once you have stalked the ball and adopted a comfortable stance, bring the mallet back slowly and begin your swing. Hold the mallet firmly, and bring it back pendulum-fashion from the mallet-head, not the top of the shaft. The swing should be flat and from the shoulders, with arms and mallet moving as one. The wrists should be flexible. The rest of your body should NEVER move during the swing. Make sure your head is immobile, as in a golf swing, and keep your eyes on the back of the ball, at the spot where you want to hit it. You should generally try to hit the ball about one inch from the bottom of the mallet-face. Keep your eyes down until the ball is well under way. It is important not to be led by your mallet in the swing, but, in Lord Tollemache's words, "to carry the mallet through." The hands and arms must control the mallet, although, again, it is swung from the shoulders. If too much wrist is used, a badly hit ball will result.

A flatter swing, when the pendulum is from the shoulders, produces a longer follow through, and results in a more accurate shot. If you find that your shot bumps at the beginning, you are probably standing too close to the ball. If it wanders from a straight line, you are standing too far away. And remember, the ball should be swept rather than hit in a definite direction. With practice, you should be able to develop a swing that is both comfortable and accurate.

ROQUER ET CROQUER.

ROQUER ET CROQUER.

Holding his mallet low and daintily swinging it between his parted spindly legs,... Pnin foreshadowed every stroke with nimble aim-taking oscillations of the mallet head, then gave the ball an accurate tap, and forthwith, still hunched, and with the ball still rolling, walked rapidly to the spot where he had planned for it to stop.
—V. Nabokov, *Pnin*

VIII
Shots

Roquet Shot

The basic shot for starting and continuing your turn is the roquet or hit shot. A roquet shot is hitting any of the other three balls (on which you are live) on the court with your own ball, thereby gaining two extra strokes. After you have roqueted another ball, you move your ball next to the one that has been struck, never the other way around. Then take the first of your two extra shots. This first shot is called the croquet or drive shot and may be taken in one of two ways. You may take it with your ball touching the roqueted ball if your plan is to drive them both in a particular direction. You may also elect to place your ball a mallet's head away from the roqueted ball, and take your croquet shot from there.

The second of the two strokes you earn by making a roquet is called a continuation shot. You may use this shot to run a wicket, make another roquet, or, simply, to improve your position. The strategic aspects of the croquet shot and continuation shot will be dealt with later. The proper way to hit a roquet shot is to imagine a straight line between the center of your ball and the center of the ball you wish to hit. Line the shot up by walking up to the ball from behind and getting a "line of aim" on the target ball. This is called "stalking" the ball, and is done the same way you would line up a putt in golf.

Many factors will determine how hard you are going to stroke your shot. If you are aiming at your teammate's ball you might want to remain very close to it, should you miss, and, therefore, you will want to make a soft shot. On the other hand, the situation might call for you to miss the roquet, and keep right on going as far as possible.

The reasons for unintentionally missing a roquet shot are the same ones that cause a dubbed shot in golf. Looking up when you hit your shot is the main cause of missed roquets. Even experienced players do it, but you've got to try to keep your head down. Another reason for missing roquets is failing to bring your eyes back up from the target ball to your ball after lining up the shot. If you are a back yard player it is best just to try to hit the target ball on your roquet shot, rather than to direct it. As you improve you will be able not only to hit the target ball but also to send it to a desired position. To do this, you will need to master the following shots:

The short rush shot.

The Rush Shot

This is a roquet or hit shot designed to move the roqueted ball a given distance in a particular direction. Any rush shot shorter than three feet is sometimes called a "short rush," while one longer than three feet or so is called a "long rush". A long rush is a tough shot, and, even on very good lawns it is handled only by the better players. But it is a fundamental part of the game and is essential to becoming a good player.

Straight Rush

This is a hit shot in which you are attempting to hit the target ball dead on rather than hitting it to one side or the other. On a short straight rush you may want to send the target ball a certain distance, so you will vary the force behind your stroke. You can do this by changing your grip, widening the distance between your hands on the shaft, or lengthening your back stroke. On a long straight rush you should only try to meet the target ball, not to send

The straight rush and the cut rush.

it a particular distance. If you are attempting to hit the target ball up to a wicket, you should not try a straight rush if this will leave the target ball blocking your hoop. Rather than hitting it straight on, you should hit it slightly off center. Another point to keep in mind is the proper stroke for the lawn conditions. When playing on a rough course, you should hit the ball on the upswing as a precaution against making your ball jump. To hit down on the ball on a rough lawn can prove fatal.

Cut Rush

This shot is used when you want to drive the target ball to the left or right rather than straight ahead. It is similar to a billiard or pool shot when you are trying to angle a ball into a pocket. In theory, you should not try a cut rush on shots greater than four or five feet but, if the playing surface is even, good players will attempt this shot at two or three times that distance. However, on medium and long range shots, you should try to hit the target ball in the middle rather than cutting it.

Running The Wicket

The big difference between making a roquet and running a wicket is with the former you are aiming at a solid object and with the latter you are aiming at a space. On a hit shot you can be slightly off and merely tick the target ball, but still, the shot is successful. When shooting for a wicket you don't have quite the same leeway. When shooting for a wicket you should try to visualize a spot right in the middle of the uprights, in the same way a field goal kicker in football would line up his attempt. Of all the basic shots, probably the one most often misplayed is the wicket shot.

Jack Osborn, U.S. player, running a wicket.

Approaching the wicket from the side, aim to clear the near upright. Approaching the wicket from straight ahead, aim to go straight through.

The principles are pretty much the same for the wicket shot as for the roquet shot:

- Do not hurry the back stroke.
- Keep an even back swing.
- Give the mallet head time to swing.

If the ball is in a good position to run the wicket, and you don't need a strong hit, hit true with just a small amount of lift. However, if you are in a good position to run the hoop, but don't want your ball to go too far past it, you should keep the mallet-head as close to the ground as possible and use a slow sweeping motion with no lift. To get the right english on the ball you should hit it at the very top, as if you were breaking an egg.

Remember that it is much easier to approach the wicket from the front, no matter what the distance, than from the side. But if you are to one side of the hoop you should hit the ball as if you are attempting a jump shot. Don't worry if you don't know what a jump shot is—we'll get to that next. If you stroke it correctly the ball will hit the upright and the english will carry it through. It's not an easy shot and virtually impossible if you're playing with flexible wire wickets.

The Jump Shot

No, this isn't something from the NBA nor is it a shot that you will see in the usual back yard game. A jump shot in croquet is hit like a wedge shot in golf, although you should be careful not to take a divot. Hitting down and behind the ball will cause it to jump. With a little practice you can get quite accurate with the shot.

The jump shot is used when you are unable to make a direct hit on a wicket or ball because one or the other is obstructing your way. Consequently you jump the obstacle.

If you want both your own ball and the target ball to go through the hoop, hit down on the ball but don't overplay it. That way, your ball, instead of making a clean jump, will mount the back of the obstructing ball and both will go through. This is sometimes referred to as the half-jump. In the regular jump shot, your feet should be well in front of the ball, while in the half-jump your feet will not be as far in front.

A sequence of photos showing the jump shot, which is used when a ball is directly in front of the entrance to the wicket. In this case, only the striker's ball and not the target ball goes through the wicket. With practice, the jump shot can be a very accurate shot and a valuable addition to the croquet player's repertoire.

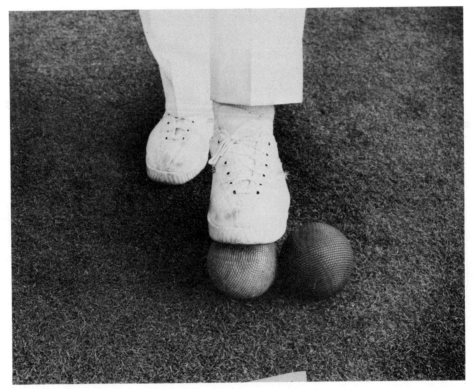

Footing the ball.

Croquet Shot

As you know, the croquet, or drive shot always follows the roquet shot. After you have made your roquet you move your ball next to the roqueted ball for your croquet shot. In advanced USCA rules and in the British game, the two balls must be touching, and the roqueted ball must "rattle" or more when you take your croquet shot. In the regular USCA rules, however, you may place your ball a mallethead away from the roqueted ball and take your shot from there. Since these rules allow for an unimpeded shot, you can readily see the advantages of taking croquet with the balls separated. You have the option, of course, of placing your ball next to the ball you've hit and then taking your shot. Or you can place your foot or your hand—yes, you can use your hand on a short shot—on your ball so that the ball remains stationary after you take the shot. This "footing" of the ball was outlawed by the British Croquet Association in 1870, and there are several local clubs in the USA that have followed their lead. Footing is not allowed in Advanced USCA but, even for the average player, this is no great

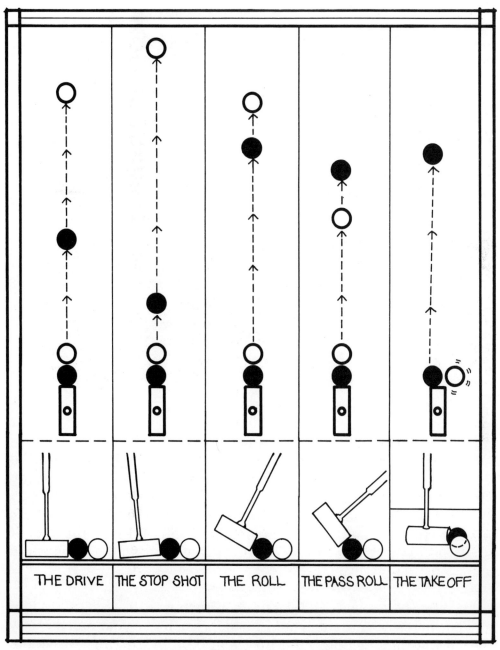

THE DRIVE | THE STOP SHOT | THE ROLL | THE PASS ROLL | THE TAKE OFF

The basic croquet shots. Note that the balls travel varying distances
and that the balls are struck differently.

handicap.

There are several basic croquet shots that you should master if
you're going to get maximum enjoyment from the sport.

69

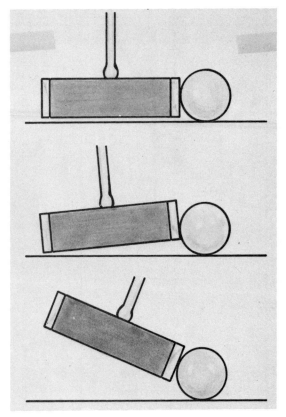

Hitting true, hitting up and hitting down.

The Hammer Shot

This is used when you are prevented from swinging your mallet because the wicket is in the way. Sometimes this shot is even taken with your back to your ball. It's a tough shot, easy to foul on, so don't worry about it unless you are a pretty advanced player. If you are forced to take a hammer shot, remember that, like the jump shot, it is not necessary to take a divot or otherwise damage the ground with your follow-through.

The Drive Shot

The drive is a croquet shot in which you place your ball directly behind the roqueted ball and hit them both in the same direction. For this shot you should assume a balanced stance, and hit your ball with the mallet-head level, using a normal follow-through. Hit the shot as if there were no other ball in front of yours. The croqueted ball should travel about three times as far as yours in a straight line.

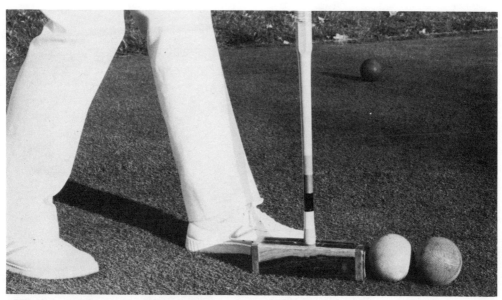

The drive shot. The mallet-head is
totally level.

The Roll Shot

In the roll shot, also known as the double roll or trundle, both balls will travel about the same distance, although not necessarily in the same direction. This is a tough shot, and to do it successfully, you should stand well over the two balls and hit down on your swing. The actual stroke is not as much a swing as it is a downward sweep. It is very important to have a follow-through with a roll shot, to give the shot enough push to allow the back ball to catch up with the front ball. If the back ball passes the front ball it is called a "pass roll." Since there is a danger of fouling on the roll shot, you should move your hands apart and keep them in advance of the mallet-head.

The Stop Shot

The object of the stop shot is to have your ball remain stationary, or travel only a short distance, while the forward ball travels a great distance. The stop shot is one of the easiest of the basic croquet shots. You should stand well back of the two balls, and in the stop shot, unlike the roll shot, you should hit with no follow-through. If played correctly, the front ball should travel up to ten times farther than the back ball. In croquet circles, a long stop shot is known as a "beefy stop shot."

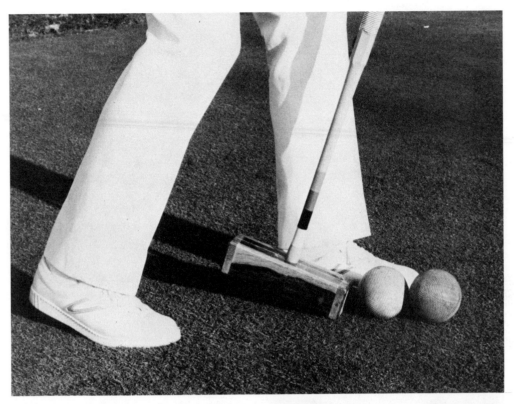

The roll shot. Observe that he is hitting down on the mallet.

The pass roll shot. Note hands and acute angle of the mallet-head.

The Split Shot

It is obvious that the distance the croqueted ball travels is determined by the angle of the split. The wider the angle, the farther

The stop shot. Note the slightly raised mallet-head.

your own ball travels because you hit less of the croqueted ball. It is very similar to splits in billiards or pool. Decide where you want the croqueted ball to end up and where you want your own ball to go, and the rest is determined by experience. The lines that the two balls will take will form an angle and to complete the split shot successfully you should "split the angle". A soft stroke is used if you want the two balls to travel a short distance, and a harder stroke is taken if you want them to travel farther. In any case, the line of aim that your mallet takes will be the same.

Ninety degrees is the widest angle for a split shot. Trying for any greater angle causes the front ball to travel a shorter distance. Keep in mind that when a split shot is made with a roll shot, there is a tendency for the balls to pull in toward each other. This doesn't occur on a stop shot because of the english used.

Remember, hitting up will decrease the length travelled by your own ball and increase the distance travelled by the forward ball. Hitting down will have the opposite effect.

The Take Off Shot

This is a variation of the drive shot. The object of the take off shot is to make the ball you hit move only a short distance while your ball goes a long way. To do this correctly, the angle formed by the mallet-head and the two balls must be slightly more than a right angle. If not, the front ball will go much farther than you intended. You should also stand over the two balls and hit down on your shot.

73

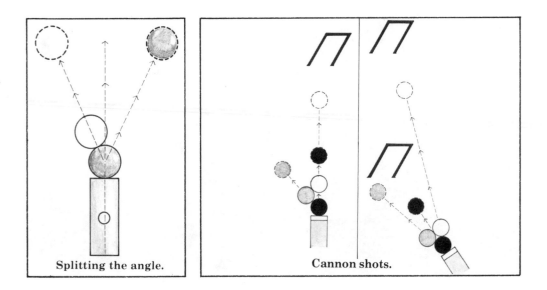

Splitting the angle.

Cannon shots.

Since the stop shot is easier than the roll shot, you should try to play with a minimum of rolls and a maximum of stops. It is easier said than done, but that should be your goal.

The Cannon Shot

The cannon shot is a shot involving three balls, and should be used by every player no matter what their level of ability. It is one of the most neglected shots in croquet, especially by American players.

There are four types of cannon shots:

The Corner Cannon

This is a combination of the rush and croquet shots and, although called a corner cannon, can be played anywhere on the court. The object of the corner cannon is to send the croqueted ball to a certain spot while at the same time your ball is hitting a third ball. As you can see, the shot can be taken anywhere on the field. Make sure when shooting a corner cannon that you don't knock the other ball out of bounds because if you do, under USCA rules, your turn ends.

Several other cannon shots, with the delightfully British names of Running Cannon, Pseudo Cannon and Kiss Cannon, are explained in the Glossary.

Another group of shots includes those in which the ball is

deliberately bounced off a peg or wicket in order to get a better position or to hit another ball. Since this shot rarely occurs when wire wickets are used, and infrequently even with the heavy iron wickets, we won't go into detail here.

The Peel

This is a shot which separates the backyard players from the serious players. A peel occurs when you cause a ball other than your own, whether on a roquet or a croquet stroke, to run its proper wicket. The peeled ball gets credit for running the hoop but gets no extra stroke, as would have occurred if the ball had been run on its own. However, if you make a peel on your roquet stroke, you get both a croquet shot and a continuation shot. Usually you would only peel your opponent's ball when you think it is possible to make it a rover, which would allow you to stake him out. If you stake him out, he is left with one ball to negotiate around the course. You must be careful not to get stuck doing the last peel with your own ball once it has become a rover. If you miss, your opponents could turn the tables and peg you out, leaving your partner to fend for himself. This last situation would not occur under British or advanced USCA rules, since only a rover can stake out a rover.

Under American rules, a peel occurs more frequently with your partner's ball than with your opponent's ball. This usually happens when your partner's ball is in the "jaws of the hoop" or is two or three ball dead and unable to roquet another ball. Peeling your partner through his wicket allows him to become alive again on all balls.

In addition to the single peel explained above, there are several other kinds of peels:

The Double Peel This is part of a standard triple peel, and it happens when a ball is peeled through two wickets on a single turn. Although the double peel occurs on a single turn, it does not necessarily occur on successive strokes.

The Triple Peel The triple peel is a move in which, as you go round with your ball, you peel your partner's ball through the last three hoops and peg both balls out. This ends the game. This is a difficult and exact series of shots, and a triple is something you rarely see, even in "A" competition.

Delayed Triple Peel Sometimes the situation arises when you might temporarily abandon the triple peel and resume it during your next turn. This move is called a delayed triple peel.

Quadruple Peel Peeling through four hoops is called a quadruple peel. It is usually seen only in doubles when assisting a weaker partner.

Quintuple Peel A five wicket peel. It rarely occurs.

Sextuple Peel This is part of a plan to finish the game in two turns, without giving your opponents a chance to hit. Several international championships have been won by using a sextuple.

The Irish Peel This is a roll shot that sends both balls through the hoop with the same stroke. It should only be attempted when you are in front of and near the hoop.

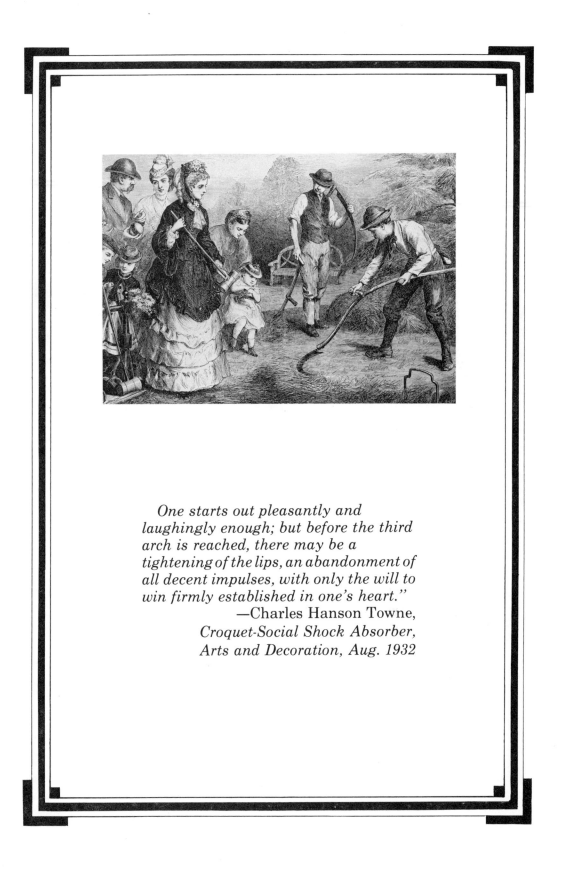

*One starts out pleasantly and
laughingly enough; but before the third
arch is reached, there may be a
tightening of the lips, an abandonment of
all decent impulses, with only the will to
win firmly established in one's heart.''*
—Charles Hanson Towne,
*Croquet-Social Shock Absorber,
Arts and Decoration, Aug. 1932*

IX
Openings

As you remember, all balls enter the game a mallet's length from the first wicket, and all are dead until they run that wicket. This rule allows you to head right for the first hoop without fear of being roqueted or leaving your opponent with the possibility of a break. Thus jockeying for opening position is unnecessary, and strategy and positional play do not really enter the game until you run the first wicket. In the British game, however, all balls are live when the game begins, and a great deal of care is necessary in your approach to the first hoop. We are including a short briefing on British opening strategy as an introduction to some of the aspects of croquet tactics which will be covered more fully in a later chapter.

If an inexperienced player were watching the start of a championship croquet match in Britain, the chances are excellent that he would rapidly become confused. For instead of shooting for the first wicket, as under American rules, the British player seemingly ignores the first hoop and, instead, shoots his balls to the side boundaries or the corners. Once you become aware of the strategy and tactics involved, this seemingly irrational behavior begins to make perfect sense.

As you gain experience, it soon becomes obvious that it is vitally important to control or be able to use as many of the balls as possible, while preventing your opponent from doing so. Gaining control of the play by superior positioning is called "getting the innings." This means that you have managed to arrange your balls in such a way that you are more likely to score points in the near future than your opponent. When you are in this position you are said to be "in."

For this reason, since the fourth ball entering the game is the one that has the best chance for an immediate break, having the other three balls on the court to shoot at, the player playing under this rule begins his game by going for the boundaries or the corners. The odds against running the first wicket from the boundary line, where British play starts, are great. Since you are already alive, if you miss that shot, you leave yourself in a vulnerable position, where you can be hit by your opponent and, hence, lose the innings. So the experienced player tries to avoid putting his balls in the center of the court, always aware of what he is leaving his foe to shoot at.

With this in mind, a basic standard opening has evolved, one that is used in nine of ten British games. In our hypothetical game, player A plays the blue and black balls and goes first. Player B plays the red and yellow balls. In opening the game player A sends his first ball, say black, to a point on the east boundary near the fourth corner. Player B sends his first ball, red, to a point on the west boundary, usually seven to ten yards from the first corner. In playing this shot, player B hopes to entice his opponent into shooting for this ball with blue, and, he hopes, missing it. This is called "laying a tice." The length of the tice is important, as the shot must appear appetizing and yet not be too easy.

Player A now has two options for his next shot. He can decide not to accept the tice and shoot blue to black on the east boundary. In playing this shot, A hopes that player B will not now hit red with his yellow ball. Player A can also decide to accept the tice, aiming if he misses to go into the second corner. He does this to prevent his opponent from doing the same. If the shot is missed, A has lost the innings, but black and blue are now near opposite corners of the court, and, hence, of little use to player B. If A does hit red, he can then take croquet and knock red to a spot where B would be unlikely to be able to hit it, such as the peg. With his continuation shot he can then send blue to join black.

Player B now shoots at red, if A has not already roqueted it. He aims for the second corner if he misses, provided that A has not already gone there. In order to do this, he must play yellow from the first corner spot. If B makes the roquet on red he has got the innings, and he can now get to the business of running wickets and setting up his breaks. If B misses the shot, A would have the innings, as his balls are together on the east boundary for an easy roquet. If player A has missed the tice and gone into the second corner, player B can shoot at red, so that, if he misses, the ball will be replaced on the yard line near yellow. If blue hits this tice, he will have the innings, and it will be difficult to seize them.

As you can see, under these British rules the opening is an important part of the game. When learning these openings, as well

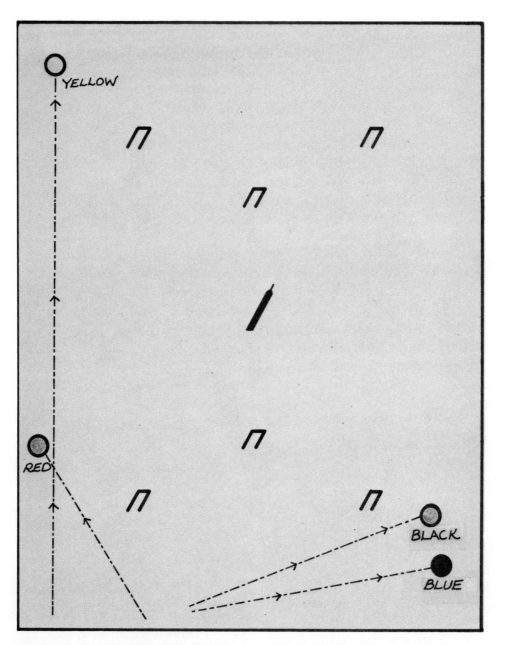

The standard British opening.

as breaks and strategy, which are covered elsewhere, it will be much clearer if you take the balls to the course and run through the opening shot by shot. The seemingly complicated maneuvering will then begin to make sense and become relatively easy to understand.

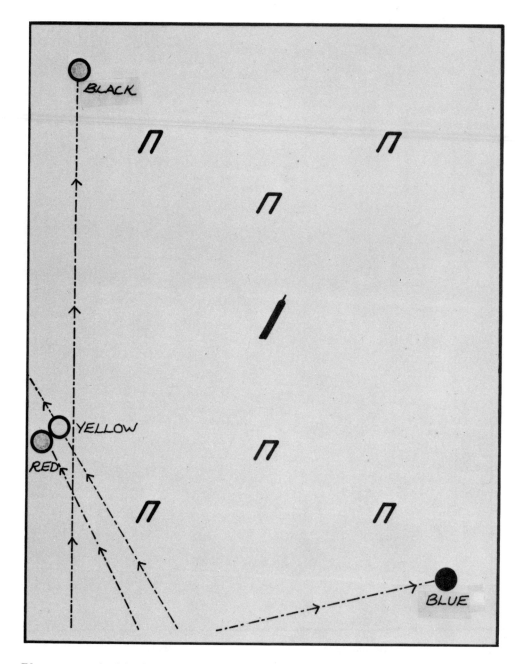

**Blue accepts the 'tice but misses and
goes on to the second corner.**

Now that we have gotten the balls into the game, it is time to go on to
the general strategy of croquet.

Blue accepts the 'tice and makes it. Blue then moves red to corner 3 on the ensuing croquet shot, and then joins up with black on the continuation shot.

*Its not the same game. Its an
absolutely different game, that's the
trouble. Its a different game and
everyone thinks its a kids game or an old
lady's game or some damn thing.*
                                    —Zanuck

X
Breaks

The good croquet player tries to place the balls in such a way that, by a combination of roquets, croquet shots, and continuation shots, he is able to make more than one hoop in his turn. Making more than one wicket in your turn is called making a break. This is a highly desirable croquet tactic. Good players are sometimes able to make all the wickets in one turn, which is called making an all round break. Breaks can be made with two, three, or four balls, but the more balls involved, the easier the break. We will discuss each type of break, and we suggest that you take the balls to the court and run through each of them, to get an idea of how they work, and to see them in action.

The two ball break is the simplest to follow but the most difficult to accomplish. Since there are only two balls involved, each shot has to be extremely accurate. One poor or off line shot will end your break. To see how the two ball break is accomplished, place two balls, say red and yellow, on the court, so that red is about two yards in *front* of the first hoop and yellow a foot behind red. You are playing yellow, and have a rush on red to the hoop. Gently rush red to the wicket so that it stops about two feet in front of the wicket and about six inches to one side. Since you have roqueted red, you now take croquet on that ball. Place yellow in contact with red so that they point to one side of the hoop, say left. With a stop shot, send yellow to about six inches in front of the hoop, with red stopping a few yards on the far side of the wicket. You can then run the wicket with yellow, making sure to hit it hard enough so that it stops just behind red. Now rush red to the second hoop. This entitles you to croquet on red. With your croquet shot, send yellow to in front of the second wicket, with red going past and to the right of that hoop. Run the second wicket with yellow, and you now have a rush on red to the third wicket. Using this same method, continue around the course. With only two balls in play, the slightest error will end your break, or at the very least, leave you with an extraordinarily difficult shot.

The pattern of sending a ball to the next wicket plus one is the basic pattern of all breaks, whether two, three, or four ball breaks. The ball that is sent to the next hoop plus one is called the pioneer ball.

The three ball break is easier to accomplish than the two ball break, since you have an extra ball to make use of, and, hence, more leeway in the accuracy of each shot. To run through the three ball break, place red and yellow as before, and add another ball, say blue, a few feet in front of the second wicket. Start the break as you did in the two ball break, approaching and running the first hoop. You now have three choices for your next shot. You can either roquet red gently, then send it with your croquet split shot to the third wicket, with yellow going to blue at the second hoop. This is a very difficult shot. You can also rush red half way to the second wicket, and attempt the split shot from this close range, or you can rush red directly to the third wicket. Take croquet from red, sending yellow to blue at the second hoop. Once you have done this, you can now roquet blue at the second wicket, approach and run it as in the two ball break. Then softly rush blue to the third hoop, and, with your croquet shot, send it to the fourth wicket so that yellow stops near red at the third hoop. If you have a perfect rush line on blue toward the fourth wicket, try to put it there on your rush shot. Then go to red at the third to make that hoop. Continue in the same fashion, sending red to the fifth wicket, and blue, after the fourth wicket, to the sixth wicket. Note the pattern of sending the ball to the next hoop plus one.

The four ball break is the easiest break to accomplish. Unlike the two or three ball breaks, the four ball break is made by making various detours around the course rather than heading right for the next wicket. Start the same as the three ball break, with black placed about three yards to the left of the stake. Run the first hoop as in the two and three ball breaks, and then roquet red gently to the third wicket. Now send yellow to black, trying to stay below black, but making sure to come within a yard or two of it. Roquet black gently and take off to blue, leaving black where it is. Now run the second wicket off blue, then roquet it gently. With your croquet shot, send blue to the fourth hoop, and yellow to black. Roquet black again, take off to red at the third wicket, leaving black near the stake, preferably a little to the right of it. Continue as before, sending the ball that you just ran the wicket with to the next hoop

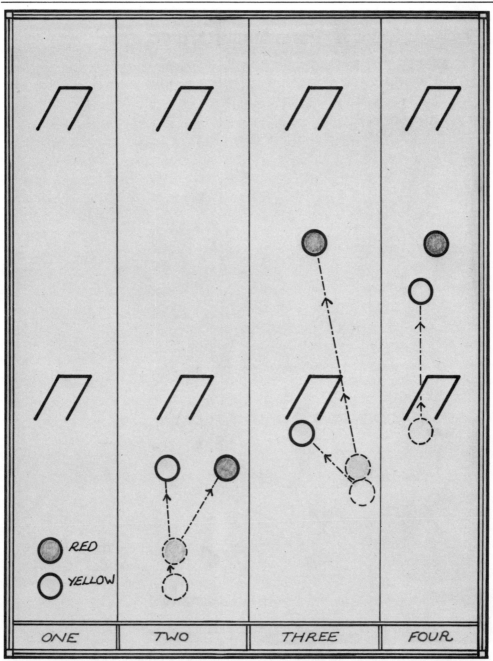

A 2-ball break. Yellow roquets red, then croquets red past the hoop, and then yellow runs the wicket himself.

plus one. This ball is the pioneer ball, and black, in this case, is known as the pivot ball. Then continue taking off from the pivot ball to the ball waiting at your next hoop.

This is the basic outline of the break. In the game, of course, you

A 3-ball break. Yellow roquets red (2), then croquets red 2 hoops ahead (3), leaving himself in a position to roquet blue. Yellow roquets blue (4), and then moves to the next hoop, with the blue ball going to the far side of the wicket (5).

Yellow runs its wicket and roquets blue again (6). On the ensuing croquet shot (7), yellow hits blue to the fourth hoop, and leaves himself with a rush on red to the third hoop.

will have to maneuver the balls into position before you can make the break, but with practice, you should be able to set up your own breaks and take advantage of those that your opponent leaves for you. Many Americans are not aware of the concept of making breaks, and, since few have practiced it, it is one of the most useful tools to learn for beginners eager to master opponents who may have played for years longer than they have.

*Do not imagine that the game is over
when you give a sigh of relief because you
are through the last hoop and have every
reason to expect that you are about to peg
out both balls. Do not relax your care by a
hair breadth until both balls have been
pegged out. There is no such thing as
shots so easy that it never has been, and
could not be, missed!"*
—Reverend G.F. Handel Elvey, 1910

XI
Pegging Out

Now we arrive at the decisive part of croquet known as the pegged-out or staked-out game. Once your ball has properly run through all its hoops, the next step for you is to peg it out, that is, to hit the final stake with your ball. If you peg both of your balls out, and do so before your opponent, you are the winner. During the staked-out game, a seemingly hopeless game can be won; likewise, a sudden defeat can be your fate. As in ordinary play, the usual basic strategic options are open to you in the pegging-out part of the game—you can shoot for the stake, play into a defensive position or bide your time until your foe shoots, hopefully misses, and places himself in a difficult position.

Don't relax and let up until both your balls are staked-out and you are the winner! Your final shots should be lined up with particular care, leaving yourself with easy rush shots to your last hoop(s). In doing this, remember not to leave yourself open as an easy target, and be especially careful not to provide your foe with a shot at both his proper hoop and at your ball. In keeping with this strategy, try to leave your opponent with only long and difficult shots.

Under certain conditions you may even find it advantageous to peg one of your opponent's balls out, and this is allowable under the rules. If you do peg out your opponent, you cut down the number of combinations he can use, and thus make it more difficult for him to keep or regain the innings. Staking-out an opponent's ball also gives you and your partner extra turns every other turn. It's a two-edged sword, of course, since *you* also lose the advantage of using the full complement of balls, and your own progress may be stalled. Remember, you can only peg-out a ball if it is a rover. In doubles, should you decide to remove an enemy ball from the game by staking it out, be sure that you peg out the better player. By so doing, you leave the fate of your opponents in the hands of the weaker foe.

Pegging an opponent out can also have the unnerving effect of disrupting your opponent's normal game, but unless you are skilled

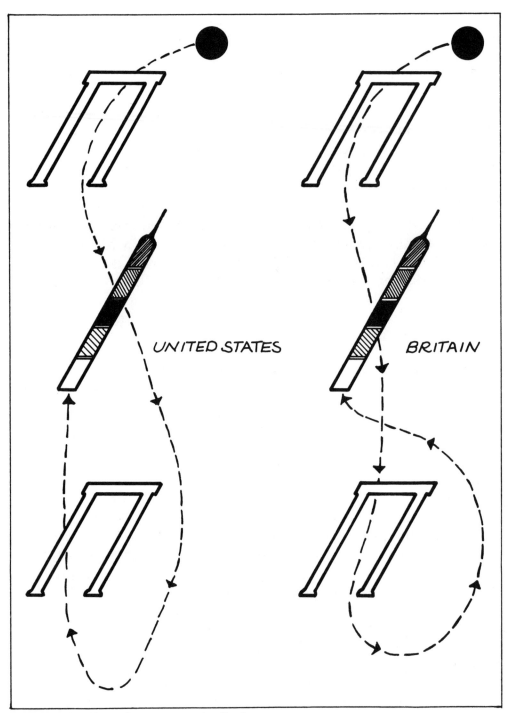

UNITED STATES

BRITAIN

Remember that when you run the final
wicket you are heading toward the
stake.

in the nuances of two- and three-ball play, it may unfortunately disturb your own style of play. Factors that will influence your decision to reduce the game to three or two balls are the comparative positions of your own and your opponent's backward ball, and your relative break-making abilities. You must also consider, when involved in a handicap game, the number of bisques which remain to yourself and your adversary.

There are many other items of strategy that you should be familiar with in order to be proficient in the two-ball game, or, games in which you or your foes have a one-ball advantage. First, consider the situation of having both balls in play, to your opponent's one. At this stage of the pegged-out game, you should try to pick up breaks whenever possible, minimizing, if you can, potential risks. In such a position, you might even try to go out on a three-ball break! Do not let your foe gain the innings, as this could have dire consequences so late in the game.

If you lack confidence in your break-making ability, try to advance just one or two hoops at a time. Try to wire your ball from your opponent whenever possible. This strategy, however, is difficult to accomplish if the lawn is uneven, as most are.

You may find that the best policy at this stage of the game is to shoot for a far boundary for defensive reasons, especially if you are unsure of your next move. This is the so-called "Thin Wire Principle," and using it sometimes entices your enemy into making a damaging move toward you, while you are in a position of relative safety.

If you have one rover, even if you are experienced and proficient in two ball play, never peg your ball out independently of your partner's ball; this avoids leaving your partner in a tenuous position. If you feel that you are suitably located for pegging both of your balls out, do not let such an opportunity pass. In any case, especially if your backward ball is ahead of the remaining enemy ball, try particularly hard to control the situation and dictate, if you are able, your foe's every move through shots of your own.

The strategy used in the situation of having one ball to your adversary's two is quite like that used in the reverse circumstances. It is, as always, crucial to prevent the enemy from undertaking a three-ball break. Be wary of going into a seemingly good position at the expense of giving your opponent a possible break. However, since it is essential for you to extend your turn for as long as you can, you must try to take advantage of all shooting opportunities. If you are shooting poorly, you can also hope to gain the innings through an enemy error. Try, if you can, to head off the enemy's lead ball.

Conversely, you can temporarily ignore your foe's position, and, instead, go for your own hoop or the stake. This might also impede your adversary's progress, as he might have to abandon his offensive game in an attempt to intercept your ball. Try, if you can, to make your final wickets on a single break, for a lapse here could prove fatal, with your foe so close to pegging-out. As in playing with a single ball advantage, with two balls you may fall back on the Thin-Wire Principle, hoping to lure the enemy into making a mistake. If you have a sizeable lead, you may decide to peg your foe's and one of your own balls out, thus beginning a two-ball game. Although some consider it questionable it goes without saying that you should not invite this situation unless your remaining ball is in a reasonable position to peg-out. Your weaponry is limited in two-ball play, but you should be able to finish out, either on a two-ball break or with single strokes.

You should consider two other factors before embarking on a two-ball game. First, do not fall so far behind that you can only rescue yourself through pure shooting. Secondly, when negotiating the difficult middle hoops, be sure not to leave yourself as a "sitting duck." When both players are going for the middle wickets, a situation similar to starting play develops, as the combatants try to creep into proper position, mutually avoiding the enemy. It often takes numerous shots to resolve this stage of the contest.

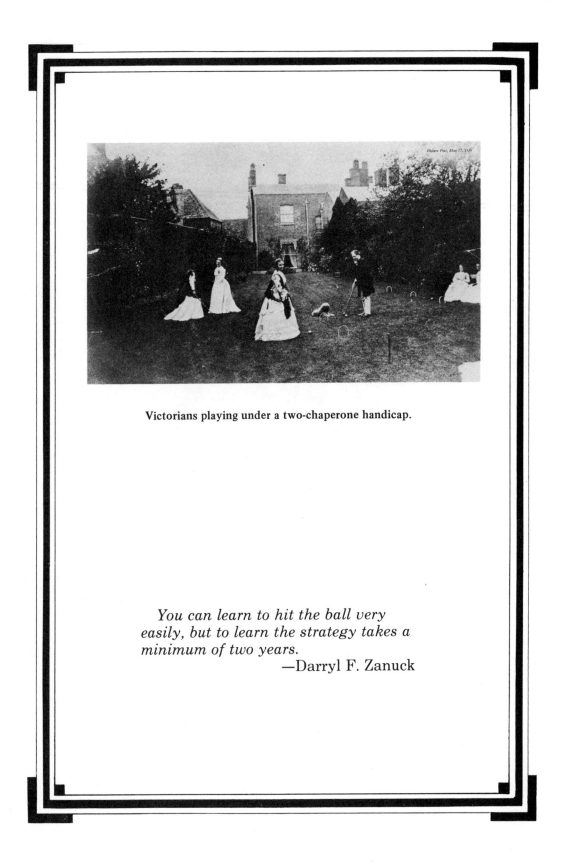

Picture Post, May 27, 1939

Victorians playing under a two-chaperone handicap.

You can learn to hit the ball very easily, but to learn the strategy takes a minimum of two years.
—Darryl F. Zanuck

XII
Handicap Play

Croquet, like many sports, uses a system of handicapping to neutralize the differences in skill between players. The unit used in croquet to express handicaps is called a *bisque,* both in American and United Kingdom play. The functions of bisques differ greatly on each side of the Atlantic.

In American tournaments, *all* players are assigned bisques, in a system usually ranging from the "scratch" player with none, to the beginner with as many as five. Bisques in American play are taken in the form of "do-over" shots. If you declare a bisque you are allowed to replace your ball to its point of origin and replay the shot last taken, provided that you are dissatisfied with the result, and have not committed a fault. You may even replace your ball and attempt a different shot. You must, when taking a bisque, use the ball that you played on your previous shot.

The English system of handicapping is much more formalized than its American counterpart, and the nature of the English bisque is quite different. The method used in British croquet is unique, for instead of using your actual handicap, as in American croquet or golf, you play off the difference between your handicap and that of your opponent. Furthermore, in England, only the *inferior* of the players or teams is allowed to use their bisques. For example, if your handicap is 3 and your foe's is 5, you would receive no advantage, but your opponent would receive two bisques. In the United States, you would get three "free" shots, and your foe would get five.

In England, bisques are not "do-overs," but rather, "free" turns, in the sense of extra shots taken at the conclusion of the preceding stroke. The English handicap system also differs in that it presently ranges from -5 (currently given to only one player, Nigel Aspinall) to 16 for the novice. Before the present limits were set, Humphrey O. Hicks achieved the greatest handicap ever, with -5½.

Bisques generally play less of a role in American play than overseas, because American players are usually more evenly matched in tournaments than their British cousins. Open events in England frequently feature matches between players of widely disparate skill, and thus the English bisque can play more of a role in the outcome. A bisque can also be more decisive under British rules, since only one player or team gets to use a handicap.

In England, a handicap unit called a *half-bisque* is used, along with bisques, in tourney competition. A half-bisque is similar to a bisque, but you cannot make a wicket on such a shot. They are generally used to improve your lie or to get out of harm's way. Some experts, including J.W. Solomon, think that bisques in singles events should be, at the discretion of the player, split into half-bisques.

In U.S. tournaments, you are expected to use the handicap assigned to you prior to the start of play. If you do not have a handicap, it is the responsibility of the tournament manager to give one to you. If you are a beginner, you should receive a handicap of at least three, or, if you are playing under British rules, a handicap of at least nine bisques. During play, the keeper of the deadness board is responsible for keeping track of the bisques.

How to Use Your Bisques

When playing in a handicap game, there are certain facts about bisque use that you should keep in mind. You should save your bisques until you are approaching the end-game, or until you are in a crucial situation. Do not waste your bisques on simply any shot—try to bisque only when the situation justifies it. Don't bisque just to advance a single wicket, for the loss of a bisque outweighs the reward of one hoop.

Once you have reached the pegged-out game, use your bisques at the first opportunity. If you are three-ball dead, and are playing under American rules, you should also take a bisque to extricate yourself.

As in level play, it is generally to your advantage to open a handicap game after your opponent. In going last, you can use your bisques with all the balls in play, and thus potentially for your use. You wish to go last in the hope of making a break and seizing the innings before your opponent has a chance to use his or her bisques.

Always assess and re-evaluate the state of the game as your bisques, or those of your adversary, are exhausted. You might improve your game in handicap play, as bisques can give you a

BRITISH SCHEDULE OF BISQUES

FULL GAME	22 PTS.	18 PTS.	14 PTS.	FULL GAME	22 PTS.	18 PTS.	14 PTS.
½	½	½	½	10½	8½	7	5½
1	1	½	½	11	9½	7½	6
1½	1½	1	1	11½	9½	8	6
2	1½	1½	1	12	10	8½	6½
2½	2	1½	1½	12½	10½	8½	6½
3	2½	2	1½	13	11	9	7
3½	3	2½	2	13½	11½	9½	7½
4	3½	3	2	14	12	10	7½
4½	4	3	2	14½	12½	10	8
5	4	3½	2½	15	12½	10½	8
5½	4½	4	3	15½	13	10½	8½
6	5	4	3	16	13½	11	8½
6½	5½	4½	3½	16½	14	11½	9
7	6	5	4	17	14½	12	9½
7½	6½	5	4	17½	15	12	9½
8	7	5½	4½	18	15	12½	9½
8½	7	6	4½	18½	15½	13	10
9	7½	6	5	19	16	13	10
9½	8	6½	5	19½	16½	13½	10½
10	8½	7	5½				

English bisque schedule. There is no
standard American counterpart.

psychological edge. Bisques can also encourage you to attempt
shots that you might ordinarily bypass. A good rule to remember is
never to "go to bed with bisques." That is, never lose a game with
unplayed bisques on your side.

One final tip—to improve your game, always try to play the
"right shot." Don't look for the easy way out. You might, at first,
sacrifice some wins because of daring play, but if you extend your
skills, have patience and practice your game, immense satisfaction
will soon be yours. You may even lower your handicap!

Handicap Doubles

Generally speaking, bisque-taking in handicap doubles is
similar to singles play. In the United Kingdom, team handicaps are

99

added together, and half the difference between the two is the number of bisques that the weaker side receives. In America, of course, all players get to use their respective bisques. In doubles, stronger players should make the tactical decisions that are in doubt, and they should gently guide the moves of the inferior partner. The best player can either stay behind to aid his partner, and then finish out with a double or triple peel when they are close to staking-out, or he can simply mirror the moves of the weaker partner and finish the course hoop to hoop.

You do not want to stray too far from your partner, in order to avoid leaving either of you in a vulnerable position. You also want your partner to be located where he can help your own progress around the course. An English rule restriction is that in some doubles handicap events you cannot peel your partner through more than four hoops. This is designed to prevent doubles matches from becoming "specialized singles," with the inferior player having little or no effect on the game.

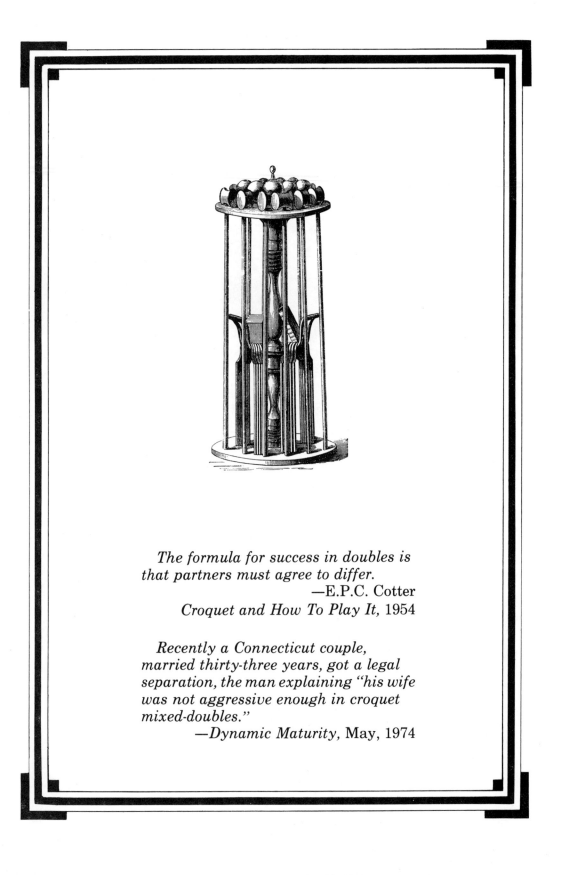

*The formula for success in doubles is
that partners must agree to differ.*
                    —E.P.C. Cotter
Croquet and How To Play It, 1954

*Recently a Connecticut couple,
married thirty-three years, got a legal
separation, the man explaining "his wife
was not aggressive enough in croquet
mixed-doubles."*
                    —*Dynamic Maturity*, May, 1974

XIII
Doubles

Even though croquet is designed to be played by two or four players, the doubles variety is considered to have some critical flaws. Chief among them is that the level of play in doubles can fall far below the individual abilities of the four players. Unless you and your partner are relatively closely matched and used to competing together, you will find that you may stray from your normal playing pattern in attempting to compensate for an inferior partner. This can downgrade the quality of play and spectator appeal alike.

Another complaint is that A-level players are frequently paired with novices, to prevent certain tandems from running away from the field. In American tournament play, however, players are generally paired more evenly than in English tournaments, so that in the States, at least, this criticism is not applicable.

Doubles croquet has essentially the same rules as those set forth for singles play. As a team, you are permitted to consult to a limited degree, but most consultation of this sort should be kept to a bare minimum—unless you are a "coarse and ill-refined" player. You are not allowed to receive advice from anyone but your partner.

As the rules for singles and doubles are similar, so too is the strategy involved, especially if all the players are fairly evenly matched. Differences do appear in tactics when the participants are mismatched, so it is crucial to keep in mind the relative abilities of your foes, as well as the skills of you and your partner.

If your side is evenly matched, try to stick to your normal approaches to the game. Decide, as a team, how the ball is to be played, and then let the striker play the ball as well as he or she can. Try to keep your inferior opponent's ball as the backward ball, with the stronger foe progressing at a faster pace so as to be susceptible to being staked-out. Needless to say, avoid leaving possible breaks, even for an inept opponent.

If you have a weaker partner, endeavor to help him or her to progress several wickets ahead of your own ball. Don't try to move too far with your ball while you are aiding your partner, as you may

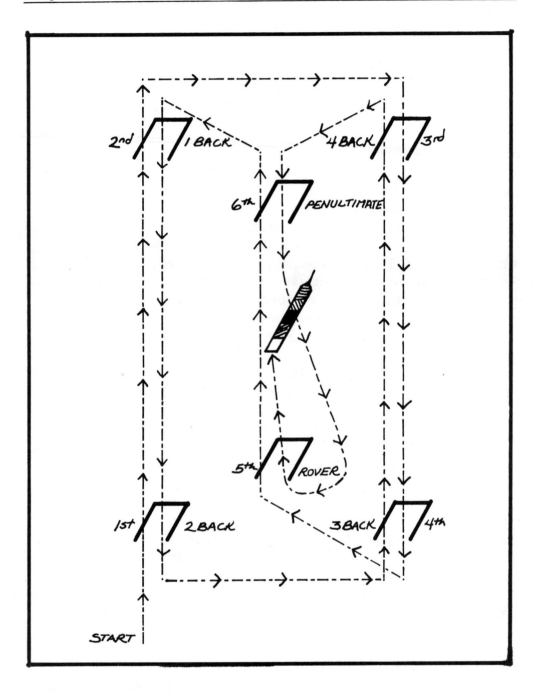

become vulnerable to being pegged-out.

In spite of the critical comments aimed at the doubles form of croquet, doubles can be exhilarating, both to play and watch. This is especially true of the major, A-flight doubles events.

CHATEAU D'EGLINGTON,

19th century French layout, with a
bell hanging from the crossed wickets
in the center.

*On my course you have to go through a
rubber tire and go round the hammock
just to get to the first wicket.*
                                    —Jim Bouton

XIV
Variations

Although the primary concern of our book is the official six-hoop game of croquet, there are, of course, numerous variations of the standard game. Some are played under the auspices of official bodies, while others are strictly on the level of "pick-up" games. In any case, no treatment of croquet would be complete without a look at the off-shoots of the parent game.

The SHORTENED GAME, either played over a course of fewer hoops, or abbreviated by a time-limit, is hardly a variation at all, in that it is essentially the same as the usual version. Although most players dislike shorter games, there are occasions when they must be used, sometimes even in serious tournament play. An over-sized entry frequently determines the use of limitations, although some tournaments only limit the participants (and raise the entry fees) to avoid shortening events. As we will discuss later, there are also instances when the lack of available space necessitates a smaller course, and thus, a shorter game. In defense of this variety of croquet it should be pointed out that it can be kinder to the spectator to watch a shortened game than for him to view inept players working interminably to end the game.

For the shortened game, the standard twenty-six point course can be altered in several ways. For a contest of TWENTY-TWO points, play starts with all players going for the third hoop. If a game is further reduced to EIGHTEEN points, play begins either with all clips on hoop five, or with all balls being for the first hoop. In the latter case, the peg-point is attempted after two-back, thus omitting hoops three-back through rover. Another method of setting up an eighteen-point game is to have the players begin with one ball for hoop one and the other for three-back.

An even shorter variety of croquet is the FOURTEEN-point game. Here the balls are put into play as if it were a regulation-length game, but you peg out after scoring the sixth hoop.

Once the course layout is settled upon, all shortened games are played under the accepted rules, with a few exceptions. There is a limit placed on the number of hoops through which you can peel your partner. Secondly, in short handicap games, the number of bisques assigned to you will be reduced in proportion to the length of the game.

In games shortened by a time-limit, play proceeds as usual, but is suspended after an arbitrary, but previously arranged time. Each player is allowed to complete his turn once the time-limit is reached.

Let us now look at croquet when it is played under the standard rules, but on a MODIFIED COURSE. In such games, the course is reduced in size to fit the existing land space. All markings and boundaries are scaled down accordingly. In extremely cramped surroundings, you should use the largest available rectangular plot of land. On such small courts, it may also be advisable to reduce the game to twenty-two points. Aside from the altered dimensions, these games are played under normal rules.

Although one naturally assumes that croquet is only a game for the outdoors, there is an officially-played INDOOR version. Since the early Sixties, in fact, croquet has been played inside under the auspices of England's stately Roehampton Club.

Indoor croquet is played on a carpet, generally no more than ten yards by eight yards in size (although there are no strictly standardized dimensions). The balls are the same as those used in snooker (small and with a very smooth surface), and only three are used. One is red, one blue and the third, considered neutral, is painted white. Only three are used for a good reason—break-making would simply be too easy in this game if the usual four balls were used.

Mallets are scaled down, but not in length. The hoops and pegs are forged from steel, and are attached by nails to floorboards under the playing carpet. Otherwise, the proportions and settings for this variety are the same as those for the outdoor game.

GOLF CROQUET, known also as CROQUET GOLF, is another interesting variation that is governed by standardized rules. This game is croquet with the hoops treated as if they were holes on a golf course. All balls are always for the same hoop, and the first to run a particular one wins the "hole," with all players then proceeding to the next hoop. Balls are played in the sequence of blue, red, black and yellow, and basically, the laws relating to ordinary play apply to golf croquet, with the following exceptions: GOLF CROQUET is a nineteen-point game, with short matches played for thirteen. In neither the short nor long versions does the peg enter into play. In shortened games you play the first twelve "holes" the normal way, but instead of subsequently pegging-out, you again play the third hoop. Similarly, this is the procedure used in the long game, but before ending the match on hoop three, you replay hoops 1-back through rover. In either form, the winner is determined in golf croquet when he amasses the majority of points.

All balls are played into the game from the boundary line. Only one stroke is allowed per player, per turn. Should you run two hoops on a single stroke, both are credited to you. If you partly run a hoop,

A 19th century indoor course in Elyria, Ohio.

you must, on your next turn, clear yourself from the hoop and make a new approach—unless you are placed there by your opponent, in which case you can make a direct attempt to score on your next stroke. The jump stroke is illegal in golf croquet.

Golf croquet, while recognized in official circles, has not gained nearly the popularity and acceptance of the ordinary game. This undoubtedly is due to its lack of strategy and variety of shots when compared with croquet.

POLO, or ROBBER CROQUET, is a short, but entertaining variety of croquet. Play starts with all balls introduced into the game from the South boundary (A-baulk line). You must run the first hoop before you are capable of scoring and making roquets. Running a hoop, hitting the peg, or making a roquet will earn you

109

an extra stroke. Running the first hoop is worth a single point, thereafter all hoops are worth two points.

You are not allowed to shoot for the same hoop or peg on two consecutive turns. When you make a roquet off an enemy ball, that ball becomes dead. The dead ball must then be re-introduced from the South boundary, and, again, run hoop one before it can score further points.

Here enters the "robber" aspect of the game, for a roquet off an opponent's ball also allows you to steal all enemy points below ten, and add them to your own total. Once you or your opponent scores ten points, those, and all subsequent groups of ten are immune from theft. Forty points wins a game of robber croquet.

One of the more bizarre varieties of croquet is the game called OFFICIAL REGULATION CROQUET. Played under the jurisdiction of the American Roque League, this game features a smooth, hard-surface court of forty by seventy-five feet, with boundaries formed by a low concrete wall. An official roque court is sometimes used for official regulation croquet as well.

This type of croquet uses a setting of ten steel hoops. These are 3-3/4 inches wide, and are nine inches above the ground. The balls are made of hard rubber, are 3-3/8 inches in diameter, and have a standard weight of twelve ounces. Official roque mallets are used.

On the relatively small course, the two center hoops are placed eighteen inches apart, and at right angles to the other wickets. The side or corner wickets are placed so that they face in the direction of the center hoops (at a 45° angle). The others face in the normal direction. The concrete wall can be used for making carom shots, a stroke peculiar to roque and this type of croquet. The wall can thus provide you with a legitimate shot, even though you appear to be unable to make a direct hit on the desired ball. The object of Official regulation croquet is to make as many hoops as possible before you relinquish your turn to your adversary.

GARDEN CROQUET is a variety that many undoubtedly regard as the true game of croquet. While some of the nine-wicket rules of the United States Croquet Association apply to the garden sport, these are basically used only as a general guide, for there is not a specific book of rules for the home game. There is no uniformity in the rules for garden croquet, and regulations are frequently adjusted to conform to local conditions and whims. Garden croquet embodies many of the assets of the usual game, but

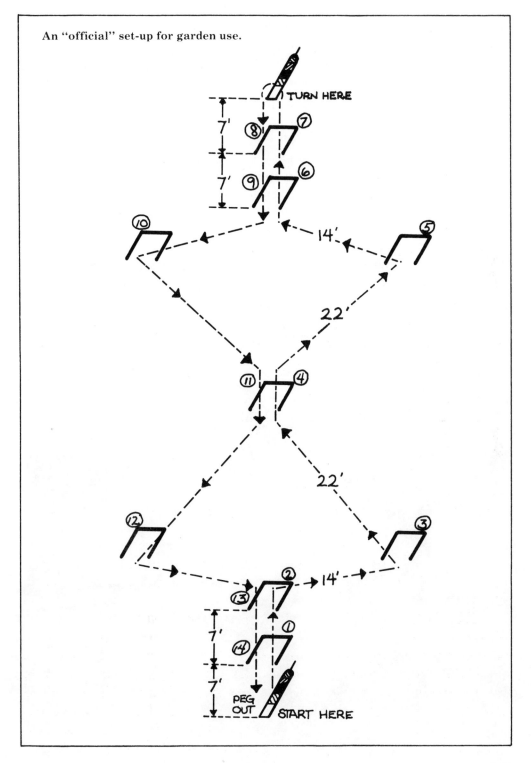

An "official" set-up for garden use.

it is neither as demanding nor as complex.

The manner in which the home course is set out is determined, obviously, by the existing space. The norm is to have as level a course as possible, but hills and natural obstacles can add spice to a home game. The size of your course is arbitrary, but many home croqueteers claim that fifty by one hundred feet are ideal dimensions. Perhaps you might also want to have areas of varying difficulty on your course.

Nine hoops and two wooden pegs are used in this variety of croquet. The boundary lines should be set roughly seven feet from the end wickets and five feet away from the side hoops. The wickets are generally made out of wire or steel rods.

Given the erratic nature of garden regulations, unorthodox wicket arrangements are permissible. You may devise spread wickets (a greater than usual distance apart), set two hoops in a

Lawn pool, one of the myriad variations of croquet.

crossed position (called a "pigpen"), or you can place the hoops in a circle. You can even do away with the boundaries if you wish.

Balls made from wood or hard rubber should be used in this type of play. The mallets can be rubber-headed or with wooden heads. The object of garden croquet is the same as for regulation play: to make as many hoops as possible during your turn.

To determine partners and starting positions, all players hit at the starting stake. Players of those balls landing nearest and most distant team up and have the choice of starting positions. Remember that turns alternate. Because of the looseness of rules, participants can be dropped or added as the game progresses, provided that all four balls remain in contention, at least until the pegging-out part of the game.

Balls are brought into play from an arbitrary point roughly midway between the starting stake and the first wicket. Basically, the rules of ordinary play are to be observed in garden croquet, but a free interpretation of the rules is permissible (and usually inevitable), making this variety an interesting and unpredictable game. Purists may pooh-pooh it, but the home version remains a widely played, heartily enjoyed form of croquet.

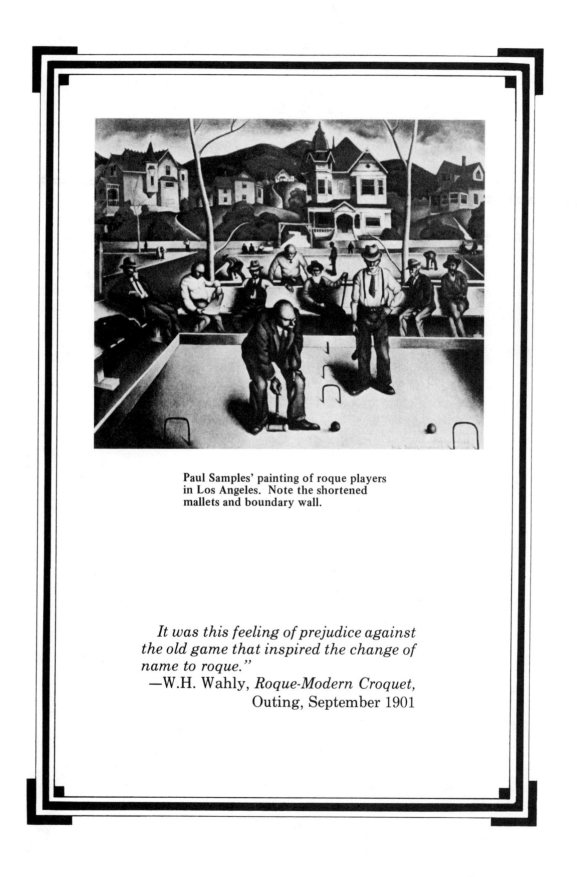

Paul Samples' painting of roque players
in Los Angeles. Note the shortened
mallets and boundary wall.

*It was this feeling of prejudice against
the old game that inspired the change of
name to roque."*
—W.H. Wahly, *Roque-Modern Croquet,*
Outing, September 1901

XV
Roque

A first cousin of croquet is roque, a North American game incorporating elements of both croquet and billiards. The American Roque League has clubs from coast to coast and has quietly and uninterruptedly been holding tournaments and crowning champions since the 1880's. Once known as the National Croquet Association, the "C" and the "t" were dropped in 1899 to differentiate between the two sports, and thus, we now have "roque."

Roque is billed immodestly as the "game of the century" and, while it may have gone virtually unnoticed by the general public, it did surface long enough to be included as an Olympic sport in 1904. Not surprisingly, an American named Charles Jacobus took the gold medal, and since roque was dropped as soon as the Olympics left St. Louis, it is one of those rare Olympic events that has never been won by a non-American.

While there are many differences between roque and croquet, the most noticeable one is that a roque court is bounded on all sides by a twelve inch high cement wall. This wall, slightly cut in at the base, is used for bank shots much like the cushions of a billiard table, and allows for variations which are impossible on a croquet court. The roque court is sixty by thirty feet, as compared to croquet's course of one hundred and five by eighty-four feet, and is sanded rather than grassy. The wickets are steel and the area between the wickets is 3-3/8 inches wide, about the same as in croquet. The balls are hard rubber and are an eighth of an inch smaller than the wicket clearance, making roque as demanding as croquet when it comes to accuracy.

The mallets used in the two sports are also different. The roque mallet has a short shaft and is usually played with one hand. One end of the mallet head is hard—usually metal—and even ivory has been used. The other end is soft rubber. Although some players use one or the other end exclusively, the rubber end is usually better for short shots and the hard end for longer hits.

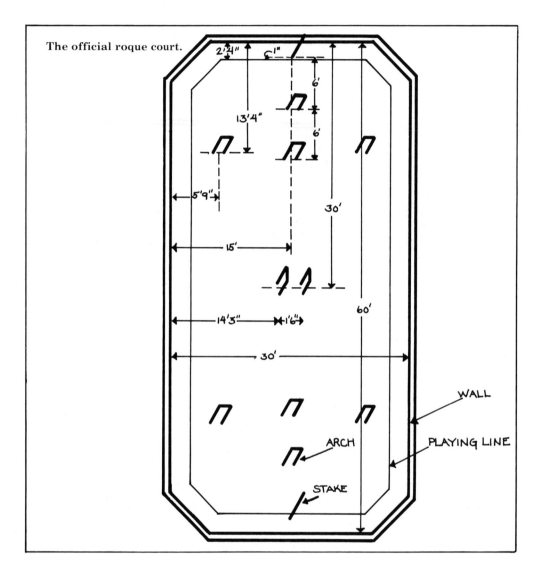

The official roque court.

Two, three or four people can play a roque game, but if three play, two players get one ball each and the third uses two balls. As with billiards, the starting sequence is determined by lagging balls toward the playing line. The order of red, yellow, blue and black is followed, but unlike croquet, the game is started by placing each of the balls at the four boundary-line corners of the court. When the game begins all balls are live on each other—unlike most American croquet variations—and, as it is virtually impossible to make a hoop on the opening shot, there are many bank shots used at the beginning of a roque game to jockey for position.

The emblem of the American Roque
League, showing roque mallets and
roque wicket.

The object of roque is to score thirty-two points—sixteen on each ball—or the most points in the allotted time. If all sixteen points ar scored on a single turn it is called a "homerun" and, since roque scores are kept by innings, the game would be over in the first inning. There are usually ten innings in a game, although tournaments often take fifteen.

Roque wickets are run differently from those in croquet. The side hoops can only be made by using the "hot ball" (the ball to be played next by your opponent) or as a solo shot, without assistance. This rule greatly reduces the chances of a homerun. The center arches are played as if they are a single arch, or they can be made in successive turns, as long as the ball stays between the hoops and does not hit a live ball. As you can see, the use of a break is especially necessary around the center.

After a ball makes all its points except the stake, it becomes a rover, as in croquet. When both partners have become rovers, the striker must complete the game by roqueting his partner's ball against the stake, and then hitting the stake with his own ball on the next shot. Incidentally, the jump shot is not legal in roque.

These are the simple outlines of a very complicated game, and it is not our intent to cover all the rules and differences between roque and croquet in one chapter. The American Roque League, now in Dallas, will provide a list of clubs, rules, a book of strategy, and even diagrams on how to construct a roque court. The best advice is to contact them before you start cementing in your back yard.

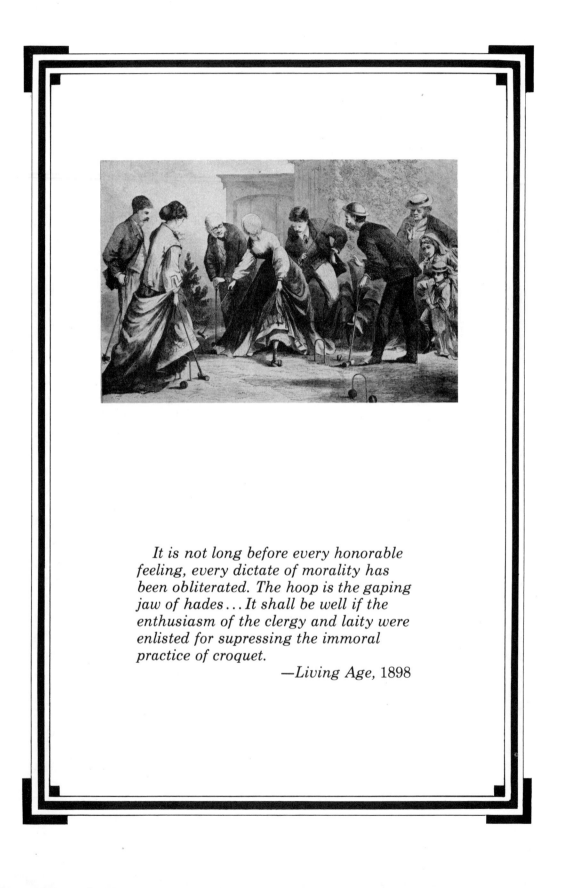

It is not long before every honorable feeling, every dictate of morality has been obliterated. The hoop is the gaping jaw of hades...It shall be well if the enthusiasm of the clergy and laity were enlisted for supressing the immoral practice of croquet.

—*Living Age*, 1898

XVI
Etiquette, Dress and Dirty Play

There is perhaps no other game with rules so precise as croquet. For this very reason, croquet etiquette is almost a redundancy: the by-laws—British or American—proscribe all but the most unseemly behavior, and the assignment of referees provides for settlements of disputes which, if not entirely amicable, at least allow the actual playing to continue.

The following, while not including specific rules or penalty-related action, should be considered important and helpful to the conduct and enjoyment of the game.

A player should not remain on the court in line of sight or area of visibility while his adversary is playing or move on to it until it is clear that he has finished or may be about to take a questionable stroke. A player should play his strokes as quickly as possible, and in doubles should avoid wasting time in prolonged discussion with his partner. (More than 90 seconds is considered excessive.)

Spectators should abstain from audible comments on the game; from offering advice to players during a game; and from calling attention to any error committed or about to be committed by any player. A spectator may reply to a question by a player on a point of fact with the consent of the adversary. A player should not take advantage of any error or omission unnoticed by himself or his partner to which his attention has been drawn during the game by the comments or attitude of spectators.

No player is entitled to advice from anyone other than his partner in doubles. It must be a matter of conscience how a player acts when in receipt of unsolicited information or advice. Warning a player other than a partner that he is about to run a wrong wicket or play with the wrong ball constitutes advice and in tournaments players and spectators are not allowed to do this.

No mark shall be made, either inside or outside the court, for the purpose of guiding the striker in the direction or strength of a stroke. A partner may use his mallet to indicate a spot, but it must be recovered before the stroke.

A player about to play a stroke, of which either the fairness or the effect (i.e. possible foul or when aiming at a ball near a wicket) may be doubtful, should suggest that a referee be called to watch the stroke. If a ball has to be replaced because of the carelessness of a player, the offending party should ordinarily defer to the opinion of the other. When the question is whether a roquet has been made on a ball or whether a ball has moved, the gentlemanly or positive opinion is generally to be preferred to the negative opinion. If there are any reliable witnesses the players should agree to consult them in order to solve differences; but no player should consult a witness without the express permission of the other player.

The striker should not test whether a ball has run a wicket by placing his mallet against the wicket without first consulting his opponent. Any such test should be made in conjunction with the opponent or if either party desires, by a referee or independent person. The same principle applies when the question is whether a ball is out of bounds, or whether it may be lifted, moved or wiped if the position of replacement is critical. All such decisions made between strokes should be made jointly.

In tournaments, a referee should always be called before a questionable stroke, and all disputes should be referred to a referee. If the opponent fails to call a referee *before* a questionable stroke, he may not afterwards appeal the decision. If the adversary believes that the striker is making faults such as "pushing" or "double tapping", he should inform the striker to have a referee called to watch the stroke.

The remarks in this section are directed to the coarse player, the man who works literally within the rules, but who is morally depraved. The following are some of his tactics.

The Psyche Out. Prior to a match, he will approach an opponent humbly and apologetically, tugging his forelock and bemoaning his own dismal health, or hangover, and inept playing style. This performance must be done deftly and with maximum sincerity, for a too-broad technique will simply not work. The opponent is to be brought only to the point of thinking he is indeed wasting his time with this amateur and of feeling sorry for him. This skillfully-induced feeling of pity and annoyance can lead to complacent play on the opponent's part. The coarse player will continue to apologize, proclaiming his great luck in making his shots, good or bad. The charade continues through the eighth wicket, at which point...

The Stall is used. This is to be employed judiciously. No shot is played until all possibilities are utterly exhausted. The proper coarse technique is to worry every potential lie (aloud), decide on a wrong shot, discover the better way, keeping up a low-pitched, nearly inaudible monologue the entire time. This monologue is crucial to the coarse player; it is masked as "thinking aloud" and if the aggrieved opponent is finally stung into saying, "For God's sake, man—shoot," an immediate reversion to the earlier humility is employed, now coupled with the hurt expression of the inferior player who is not being given a chance to play a decent game against a ferocious opponent. The coarse player will immediately ask the referee if any breach of time has taken place; the tone of voice will suggest harassment and persecution.

He will, of course, start reminding his opponent of *his* passing time immediately after time has been called. If an opponent is allowed 75 seconds to stalk or plan the next shot, the coarse player will start displaying his impatience after 30 seconds or so. Naturally, this is not done with any petulance, but with the righteousness of his avowed belief that the 90 seconds had expired.

By now the opponent of the coarse player may be angry enough to misplay. Under no circumstances will he be advised prior to making his shot. However, should he play on a dead ball, he will be so informed after the shot, in a helpful, solicitious voice, tinged with true regret.

The throwing of the mallet should always be up in the air. It should never be directed at an opponent, referee or onlooker.

The coarse player will usually appear late for a match and will never apologize for his tardiness. He may even inquire as to why people are standing around. Should he arrive before his opponent, he will, of course, either accuse his opponent of deliberately holding up beginning play by addressing loud remarks to the gallery about the virtues of punctuality, the essential bad manners of late comers, etc. The remarks will never be directed to the opponent, but should be made in his hearing.

If this tactic is too aggressive or the opponent has a volatile temperament (see reference to mallet throwing), sly suggestions as to fear causing lateness can be brought into play.

121

Since croquet garb is generally informal, the coarse player might appear in a business suit or dinner clothes, wearing them with the air of one who has more important things to do.

When the opponent is stalking his ball, the coarse player will try to make a distracting sound of maximum irritation. Popping gum, cracking knuckles, sucking teeth and whistling are all examples of noises which have turned coarse players into champions. Concurrent with the noise ploy, remarks to the gallery regarding the extraordinary improvement X is showing in his game and his great luck should also be made. The suggestion that he is playing above his head today is the most effective, as is half-hearted applause after an adequate but not difficult shot. Applause is never to be used when a truly fine shot is made—the coarse player did not see it. The suggestion—only suggestion—is that there is some trickery involved.

In the opening wickets, the coarse player will use destroy shots and approaches as often as possible.

Coarse players are a fact of croquet life, and while it is natural to deplore this playing style, the new player should be aware of this streak of ferocity in order to guard against it.

DRESS

The proper croquet garb, like the game itself, is determined by quiet good taste. There are of course bespoke, chic làbels seen more and more on trendy courts and these are accepted without comment, but essentially the rules for dress are flexible; limited only by practical rules of comfort. The game is a demanding one, and as such demands a comfortable uniform. Freedom of motion is the ultimate criterion.

Shoes

Out of consideration for the course, the croquet shoe should be soft and flat soled. The soft rule is a good one; not only is the course protected but the player is guaranteed maximum foot comfort for the grueling hours ahead. Whether the shoe is a Gucci slip-on, a Topsider, Adidas sneakers or disreputable jogging shoes is determined by the breeding and personal preference of the individual. Champion players have been known to favor all varieties, with a surprising number opting for the disreputable, albeit well broken-in, tennis shoe. Indeed, some in the U.S. have played barefoot. Style must be sacrificed only insofar as protection of the playing surface is concerned. Shoes with sharp heels are not to be worn under any circumstances during play.

The Shirt

Skillful players at any level will take every advantage to improve their game. Many croquet buffs believe the generously cut shirt provides a more fluid swing and so recommend wearing a shirt a size larger than normally worn. Opponents of the bigger-shirt theory hold that the extra material may in fact impede the swing by increasing wind resistance; logically, they extend their thinking by wearing snug, wrinkle-free pullover short-sleeved shirts, preferably of a synthetic material. The synthetic fabric, according to these theorists, will not absorb moisture and will therefore be of lighter weight during the course of the play. Too, they feel the synthetic fabric will move more freely through the air.

It's an argument that has gone on for some time, and the rule book for croquet sensibly ignores it. A shirt or top (particularly for women players) should be worn; the style and fabric to be chosen and determined by one's own standards of playing comfort.

English traditionalists ask that the croquet shirt remain a white broadcloth Sea Island pima cotton, the long sleeves rolled to just below the elbow.

The Trousers or Skirt

White flannel is still worn by serious players in England, and it is hard to fault the elegance of this classic garb. However, in croquet, alas like in too many things, standards have changed over the years and skirts and trousers of every conceivable cut and fabric are now seen on the croquet court. Croquet players, like all athletes, have their superstititions. In consequence, the "lucky" blue-jeans, flannels or shorts will be worn repeatedly. There are known instances of players being requested to change their luck and their trousers, but again, the rules are wisely flexible in this regard. The selection of color, fabric and cut of skirt or trousers remains the exclusive province of the wearer.

Head Gear

Fortunately for civilized play, the protective helmet is no longer needed. At one point in croquet's checkered history, the mallet was used as imaginatively as today's hockey stick, a flexibility that encouraged the wearing of leather caps not too dissimilar from the football helmet. Happily or not, these are bygone days.

The billed cap is to be worn only for protection against the heat and glare of the sun. An attempt at a team uniform—to include the visored cap emblazoned with team colors—simply did not catch on. Frankly, caps are considered effete by seasoned players, and are openly discouraged except when playing in the tropics or Australia.

Socks

White, of cotton or wool, is the preferred color sock. The sock should reach well above the ankle, but need not reach mid-calf. Croquet is nothing if not a realistic game. Many players do not wear socks at all.

Foul Weather Croquet Gear

One of the hardier games, croquet provides for continued play even in the face of inclemency. Since a game will not be delayed until puddles begin to form on the court, players are advised to make provision for playing in the rain.

The standards for rainwear are simple: usually a large umbrella held over the head of the player by his partner. Boots and raincoats are generally not worn since they act as obvious impediments to a clean swing. There are no specifications regarding the size or color of the umbrella, but a player is under no obligation to share or to offer to share an umbrella with an opponent foolish enough not to provide for the vagaries of the weather.

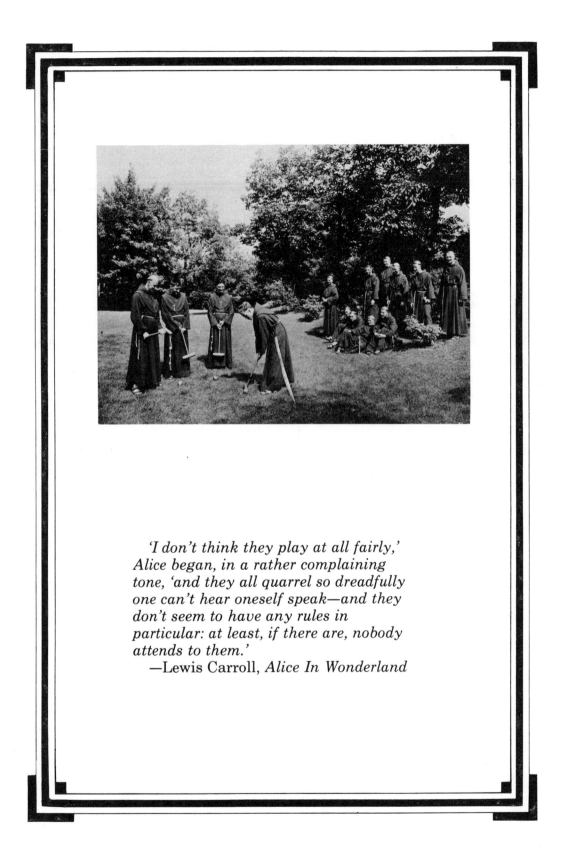

'I don't think they play at all fairly,'
Alice began, in a rather complaining
tone, 'and they all quarrel so dreadfully
one can't hear oneself speak—and they
don't seem to have any rules in
particular: at least, if there are, nobody
attends to them.'
—Lewis Carroll, *Alice In Wonderland*

XVII
Rules

THE COURT AND SETTING, EQUIPMENT AND COURT ACCESSORIES

The Standard Court

The Standard court is a rectangle, measuring 35 by 28 yards. Its boundaries shall be marked out clearly, the INSIDE edge of the definitive border being the actual boundary. Nylon string or plastic tape stapled or otherwise affixed to the ground can be used for boundary lines.

Court References

The four corners of the court are known respectively as Corners 1, 2, 3, and 4. The four boundaries are known as the South, West, North and East boundaries—regardless of the orientation of the court.

The Standard Setting

The stake shall be set in the center of the court. The wickets shall be set parallel to the North and South boundaries; the centers of the two inner wickets 7 yards to the north and south of the stake; the centers of the four outer wickets 7 yards from their adjacent boundaries. This is preferred court size and setting for major tournaments.

Modified Court Size and Setting

Should the area be too small to accommodate a standard court, a modified court may be laid out in accordance with the above by maintaining the same proportions of five length units long by four length units wide but using a smaller modified length unit. EXAMPLE: Units of ten feet could be used to set the court dimensions. Thus 40 feet wide x 50 feet long with the stake set in the middle at the intersection of the two diagonals is a possible set up.

The corner wickets are 1 unit (10 Feet) from their adjacent boundaries. The center wickets are 1 unit (10 Feet) in each direction from the stake. Local conditions may require other layouts, but the size above is generally considered the minimum for this game.

EQUIPMENT

Wickets
The wickets shall be of round iron 5/8 inch diameter and of uniform thickness. They shall be 12 inches in height above the ground measured to the top of the wicket, vertical and firmly fixed. The crown shall be straight and at right angles to the uprights, which shall not be less than 3-11/16 inches or more than 4 inches apart uniformly between the uprights (inside measurement) provided that all wickets on any one court shall be of the same dimensions. The wickets shall be painted white, the crown, of the first wicket colored blue, and that of the last wicket which is known as the rover wicket, red. (This style of wicket is used in major tournaments.)

Another form of light weight iron wicket (sometimes referred to as 'winter wickets' since they can be set into hard ground more easily) is 7/16 inch in diameter with 4 inches between uprights. It is also used in non-tournament games where circumstances or conditions warrant.

The Stake
The stake shall be of wood, of a uniform diameter above the ground of 1-1/2 inches. It shall be 18 inches in height above the ground, exclusive of a detachable portion to hold clips, vertical and firmly fixed. The base shall be painted white with blue, red, black and yellow bands descending in that order from the top.

The Balls
The balls shall be colored respectively blue, red, black and yellow. They shall be 3-5/8 inches in diameter and of even weight, not less than 15-3/4 ounces nor more than 16-1/4 ounces. Faulty or damaged balls may be changed during play.

Mallets
The head of the mallet shall be of wood, or any other material, provided that the player shall gain no advantage over wood. Metal

may be used for weighting or strengthening it. The two faces shall be parallel and identical in every respect. There may be a bevelled edge which shall not be considered as part of the face.

COURT ACCESSORIES

The following accessories should be supplied for guidance, convenience and decoration. The accessories do not form part of the setting of the court. Accordingly, any such accessories impeding a striker may be temporarily removed.

Corner Flags

Flags colored blue, red, black and yellow, shall be placed on corners 1, 2, 3, and 4 respectively. The flags shall be mounted on pegs about one foot high. The pegs shall be touching the boundary but no part shall be on the court. These are used primarily as an aid in judging distances and are not essential to the game.

Extension to Finishing Stake

A detachable portion to hold the clips shall be attached to the top of the stake.

Clips

The function of clips is to indicate the state of the game on the court. The wicket or stake next in order for every ball at the beginning of every turn shall be distinguished by a clip of color corresponding with that of the ball. When a ball scores a wicket, the striker shall remove the clip at the end of the turn, and place it upon the appropriate wicket or the stake. When the stake is scored the clip shall be removed from the court. The first six wickets shall be distinguished by placing the clip on the crown of the wicket, the last six by placing it on one of the uprights. Each player and/or referee should call the attention of the other to a misplaced clip as soon as the mistake is observed, and the clip should then be properly placed.

It is also permissible and desirable that a check-fence just high enough to arrest the progress of balls, be placed round the outside of the court about a yard from the boundary.

Deadness Board

In order to aid the contestants (and spectators) in remembering the balls they are dead on, a white board approximately a yard square with the four ball colors permanently affixed in proper sequence either horizontally along the top or vertically on the left side and 12 colored discs (three each of the four ball colors) to be hung on nails or hinged wooden markers and able to be flipped up and down. These are arranged in four columns (one column per ball) so that they may be exposed as each ball's deadness occurs and removed from view when that ball's deadness ends.

INTRODUCTION TO THE
AMERICAN SIX-WICKET CROQUET GAME

THE OBJECT OF THE GAME

Singles
The singles game is played between two players—one of whom plays the blue and black, the other the red and yellow balls. The object of the game is for a player to make both of his balls score the 12 wicket points and the stake point, a total of 26 points, before his adversary.

Doubles

The doubles game is played between two sides, each side consisting of two players. One team plays the blue and black balls and the other the red and yellow balls. Each player plays the same ball throughout the game. As in singles the object is to have one team score the total of 26 points before their adversaries.

In Both Games

A ball scores a wicket point by passing through the wicket in the order and in the direction shown on page 104. This is known as running a wicket. But a ball which has first hit another ball (roqueted) cannot thereafter *in the same stroke* score a point for itself, except at the first wicket as in Rule 9. A ball which has scored all 12 wicket points is known as a rover. It can then score the stake point by hitting it. In time limit tournament games, wicket (and stake) points are added at the end of the game and the team with the most points is the winner.

How Play is Made

Play is made by striking a ball with a mallet. The player so playing is called the striker, and the ball which he strikes, the striker's ball. The striker may never strike an adversary's ball with his mallet. By striking his ball the striker may cause any other ball to move and/or to score a point.

The Turn

The players play each turn in sequence (blue, red, black and yellow). A player is initially entitled to one stroke in a turn, after which his turn ends unless in that stroke his striker's ball has scored a wicket point or hit another ball. When the wicket is scored the striker is entitled to play one additional or continuation stroke. When another ball (whether opponent's or partner's) is hit, the striker is said to have made a roquet on that ball and he becomes 'dead' on that ball and is entitled to two extra strokes.

The first of these two strokes is known as the croquet stroke, and is made after moving and placing the striker's ball in contact with or up to one mallet head away from the roqueted ball which, if placed in contact with the ball hit in the croquet stroke, is known as the croqueted ball. If, in the croquet stroke, the croqueted ball is sent off the court or the striker's ball is sent off the court without first having made another roquet, the turn ends. During a turn the striker may roquet each ball he is 'alive' on once, and he may make a further roquet on each ball provided that since he has last roqueted it, his striker's ball has scored a wicket point for itself and has thus cleaned itself of it's "deadness". Thus, by a series of strokes entitling him to continue, the striker may make one or more points during one turn. Such a series is known as 'making a break'. But continuation strokes are not cumulative so that a striker who:

(a) first scores a wicket and hits another ball in the same stroke may either take one additional (continuation) strcke and not be dead on the ball so hit, or roquet the ball and take two;

(b) makes a roquet in a croquet stroke immediately takes croquet and continues accordingly;

(c) scores a wicket for his striker's ball in a croquet stroke plays only one continuation stroke;

(d) scores two wickets for his striker's ball in one stroke plays only one continuation stroke.

Ball in Hand

A ball in hand is any ball which has to be moved, and is therefore lifted and given a fresh position on the court in accordance with the Rules i.e.:

(a) a ball which has made a roquet;

(b) a ball off the court;

(c) a ball lifted under Rule 13;

(d) a ball which has to be re-positioned after a fault or irregularity.

Ball Off the Court

A ball off the court is a ball in hand as soon as it goes off the court, which is when its vertical axis crosses the boundary line (more than half way over).

Replacement of Balls off the Court
and Near Boundaries

After each stroke all balls off the court shall be replaced one mallet head in from the point where they went out. At the end of each turn all balls less than a mallet's head off the boundaries are replaced that length from the line.

STRATEGY

Along with the basic objective of scoring the 26 points first, each team or player (in singles) should employ those offensive or defensive moves which will restrict the progress of the opponents.

PART 1—USE OF THE MALLET

1. A player must hit the ball with the striking end of his mallet head. He may hold any part of his mallet-shaft with one or both hands, and may use any stance he wishes so long as he does not rest his hand, arm or shaft of the mallet on the ground.
2. A ball must be struck and not shoved.
3. It shall be counted a stroke if in the course of striking his ball a player's mallet hits a wicket but not the ball, or if he drives his mallet into the ground without contacting the ball; or misses it entirely.
4. If a ball lies so that a player cannot strike it squarely, he may not place another mallet against the ball and hit that mallet with his own, nor may he, if his ball is frozen to a wicket, hit the wicket to make the ball move.
5. In the course of the stroke a player may strike only his own ball without touching another ball with his mallet. For penalty see Part 9, Rule 56.

PART 2—STARTING THE GAME AND WICKET NO. 1

6. The toss of a coin determines the starting order of play. The side winning the toss has the choice of playing first and third with blue and black or second and fourth with red and yellow.
7. All balls must start from the starting-tee in the order shown on the stake (blue, red, black, yellow) and must continue in that order throughout the game, or until put out of play. The starting tee may be marked one mallet's length behind the first wicket by two coins or markers one mallet head apart. The ball must be played from between the markers.
8. Each ball is dead until it has made No. 1 wicket (the blue crown wicket).

9. A player who has not made No.1 wicket may drive his ball and hit any other ball which has likewise not made that wicket, so as to put it into position, out of position, or through the wicket. This ends his turn unless his ball also makes a clear passage through the wicket, which entitles his ball to one additional stroke. The other ball which has thus been put through the wicket shall be considered to have made the wicket but is not entitled to an extra stroke.

10. A player who drives or caroms through No. 1 wicket is deemed to have made the wicket, and is entitled to one extra stroke, but is nevertheless dead on all balls which have not made this wicket.

11. A player who drives or caroms through No. 1 wicket and in the same play then strikes a ball which is not itself through that wicket is not penalized. The other ball is replaced, and then he receives one additional stroke.

12. If the space to which such a ball should be replaced is then occupied by another ball, the replaced ball shall be put a mallet-head in any direction from the said ball at the discretion of the opponent, but not through the wicket.

13. A player who has made No. 1 wicket may hit only those balls on which he is alive.
A ball which has not made No. 1 wicket and which lies in the intended path of any ball which is through that wicket may be lifted and replaced after the stroke of the ball in play (i.e. a ball for wicket No. 2 back may lift and after his stroke replace the one which has not made No. 1).

PART 3—MAKING A WICKET

14. A ball must make a complete passage through a wicket in the proper direction, and is considered through the wicket if a mallet-head, when placed across the approach side of the wicket, does not touch the ball.

15. A ball stopping in the wicket, or one which goes through but rolls back into it, has not made the wicket.

16. If a ball is for a wicket but on the wrong side, it may be played through the wicket to the approach side, but it must clear the wicket on the non-playing side in order to be played through subsequently.

17. A ball which is dead on another ball lying at or partially in the approach to wicket (except prior to No. 1 wicket), may not hit that ball in trying to make the wicket. If it does, the wicket is not made and the player's turn ends, with his ball and the ball so hit being replaced. However, a player may use the jump shot to make a blocked wicket, a blocked stake, or at any time.

18. A ball which is dead on another ball lying beyond (not intruding into) a wicket must make a complete passage through the wicket, either before or after contact, if any, to be alive and receive one extra stroke.

19. A ball running a wicket other than one in the proper sequence or direction shall not receive credit for that wicket, except if it is a rover. See Part 8 Rule 41.

20. A player may block a wicket for one turn in addition to the play of blocking; on the next turn he must leave the wicket clear for the opponent's next turn or be lifted and replaced after that turn.

21. Upon making his first wicket of a turn, a player should remove his clip, and at the end of his turn attach it to his next wicket. For the first six wickets the clip is placed on the crown, thereafter on one of the uprights. Each player, referee or official scorer should call attention to a misplaced clip, which should then be properly placed.

PART 4—ADDITIONAL STROKES

22. A player making a wicket in the correct sequence receives one additional stroke in any direction. EXCEPTION: Part 7, Rule 39.

23. A player who hits a ball on which he is alive receives two additional strokes. EXCEPTION: Part 9, Rule 51.

24. A player who makes his wicket and hits a ball on the same play must hit that ball again to receive two extra strokes from it. He may, however, use his one additional stroke if he prefers and shall not be considered dead on that ball. In both cases the ball hit is not replaced.

25. The use of extra strokes:
    a) After hitting a ball on which he is alive, a player must either:
       1) bring his own ball a mallet head or part thereof from the one hit, and play two strokes from there; but he may

not place his own ball through or under a wicket,

or 2) place his ball against the one hit and hold it by foot or hand while driving the other away, and then play his second stroke,

or 3) place his ball against the one hit and play a croquet stroke and then his second stroke.

b) Under no circumstances may a player, in making any of the above shots, place his ball out-of-bounds.

26. Any player may handle any ball which is replaceable after contact, or may return any ball which has made a roquet to its player without penalty. A player may place a ball for his partner's croquet stroke to save time, and may give a temporary aiming mark. A player may lift his ball to clean it at any time during the game. Any ball accidentally moved shall be replaced without penalty. EXCEPTION: Part 9, Rule 56.

PART 5—BISQUES

27. A bisque is a handicap stroke wherein the striker is allowed to replay a shot from its original position on the court. A bisque may be taken only if the ball can be replaced accurately, by having marked the ball with a coin (directly behind the ball). within a mallet head of a roqueted ball or the boundary line. The intention of taking a bisque need not be announced before the original shot is made.

28. A bisque may be taken for only the immediately preceding stroke.

29. A bisque may not be taken if the original shot resulted in a penalty; for example out-of-bounds, hitting a dead ball, or striking the wrong ball.

30. A player may not take more than one bisque per turn.

31. In doubles tournaments the players will individually play with their full quota of bisques (i.e. a 2 handicap receives two bisques for his ball only).

32. In singles tournaments a player plays *only* his handicap quota for both balls. (i.e. 2 handicap receives two bisques total which can be used for either ball, or both taken on one ball).

PART 6—DEAD BALL

33. When a striker's ball hits another upon which it is alive, it is

immediately dead on that ball until the player has made his next wicket, but he may play off it as in Part 4, Rule 25. EXCEPTION: When the striker's ball hits a ball out-of-bounds, his turn ends, but he remains alive on that ball, which is replaced one mallet head in from where it went out.

34. If a striker's ball directly hits a ball on which it is dead the striker's turn ends and both balls shall be replaced. EXCEPTION: During a croquet stroke, the ball being croqueted may be hit more than once by the striker's ball without penalty. (e.g.: twice during a split or trundle shot).

35. If a ball roquets one on which it is alive and thereafter during the same stroke hits another ball, whether alive or dead on it, the latter shall be replaced without penalty (i.e. no penalty if out-of-bounds, or credit for wicket or stake). The player must play off the first ball hit and is not dead on the second ball if originally alive on it.

36. If during a croquet shot the player's ball strikes another ball on which it is dead, the turn ends, and the ball just hit and the striker's ball are replaced. If, however, in a croquet shot, the player's ball strikes a ball on which it is alive, it has then made a roquet on that ball and must play off it as in Part 4, Rule 25.

37. Any third or fourth ball struck (cannoned) by a roqueted or croqueted ball (whether alive or dead on it) will be treated as having been played directly, with all balls remaining where they lie at the end of the stroke. The struck ball, given credit for wicket or stake if made, and no deadness is created between the roqueted or croqueted ball and the cannoned ball. If no fault has occurred, the striker may then take his next stroke. If any ball (except the striker's on a roquet stroke) goes out-of-bounds, the striker's turn ends, all balls remain where they lie, and the out-of-bounds ball(s) is replaced on the boundary where it went out.

PART 7—ALIVE BALL

38. A ball becomes alive upon being driven through its wicket.
39. A ball knocked through its wicket by a striker's ball which is:
    a) *alive* on it, shall be considered alive and through the wicket, but is not entitled to an extra stroke;
    b) *dead* on it, is not considered to have made the wicket, and both balls are replaced.

PART 8—ROVER AND FINISHING THE GAME

40. A player who has made all the wickets in the proper sequence becomes a rover and is considered alive on all balls upon making No. 12 wicket (the red crown wicket).

41. To become alive a rover may go through any wicket in any direction, receiving an extra stroke. If the ball does not clear the wicket, it must, unless knocked out, continue through in the same direction in order to be considered clean.

42. A rover ball may hit any other ball only once per turn. Before clearing himself he must be dead on at least two balls, but nevertheless, he remains temporarily dead on the ball last hit before clearing, until he hits a different ball, whereupon this temporary deadness disappears.

43. A rover ball driven to the stake, either directly by himself or by a ball which is alive on it, is considered to have finished the game and shall be immediately removed from the court.

44. A rover ball driven to the stake by the striker's ball which is dead on it shall be replaced and considered still in play.

45. A rover ball hitting the stake afer a roquet is not staked out and shall play normally off the roqueted ball.

46. When one ball has finished the game it loses all subsequent turns, is removed from the court immediately, and the next ball in rotation plays.

47. If in a roquet shot the striker drives a rover ball to the stake, it is removed from play and the striker receives two strokes taken a mallet head in any direction from the stake.

48. The game is won by the side who finishes the game with both balls first.

PART 9—FAULTS AND PENALTIES FOR OUT-OF-BOUNDS, PLAYING OUT OF TURN, PLAYING WRONG BALL, UN-FOOTING BALL, ILLEGAL SHOTS AND CONDONED PLAY

49. A ball is out-of-bounds when its vertical axis crosses the boundary line (more than halfway over). It shall be replaced one mallet-head, approximately nine inches, from where it went out, or, if near a corner, at least one mallet-head from both boundary lines.

50. At the end of every turn, any ball less than one-mallet-head from the boundary shall be placed one mallet-head from the boundary line (nearest to its original position).

51. If a striker sends any ball at any time out-of-bounds, his turn ends. EXCEPTION: If, during a roquet, the striker's ball either goes out or caroms into a third ball sending the latter out. (Also see Part 6, Rule 33.)

52. If a ball is played out of turn, all balls are replaced as at the beginning of play, and play is resumed in proper sequence with the offending player losing his turn in that sequence.

53. If, in making a foot or hand shot, a player's ball loses contact with his foot or hand, his turn ends, and both balls remain where they lie.

54. A player will commit a fault a) when after making a legal roquet, he plays his next stroke from a distance greater than one mallet head from the ball hit, or b) if, after failing to properly replace his ball on the boundary line (at the end of the preceding turn), he plays his ball from less than a mallet-head from the line. The penalty is the end of player's turn, all balls are replaced to where they were before the fault occurred, no credit given for wicket or stake nor deadness created on any ball hit on that stroke.

55. If a player plays the wrong ball, his turn ends and all balls are replaced to where they were before the fault occurred.

56. If a player, in attempting to strike his own ball, touches (with his foot or mallet) another ball, his turn ends and both balls are replaced.

57. A fault or misplay by a player must be called by his opponent before the next turn begins or else it will be automatically condoned.

58. If a player makes any stroke or strokes as the result of any false information concerning the state of the game supplied by his adversary, he shall have the right to replace and replay these strokes, providing that his claim is made before the end of the offending team's next turn.

PART 10—REFEREES

59. The role of the referee is to resolve disputes between the players by reference to the book of rules. Any situation which does not

appear to be covered by these rules shall be decided by the best judgment of the referee.

60. A referee should not intervene unless asked by the players. EXCEPTION: Rule 21 (re: clip replacement).

61. In the absence of an appointed referee, the players will act as their own joint referees, but there is an obligation on the adversary to watch the game, and if he fails to do so, the striker is, during such period, the sole referee. In doubles, all players share the rights and duties of a referee, and a reference to the striker includes his partner.

62. If, during a tournament match, a player fails to request that an adversary call a referee to observe a questionable stroke before it is taken, he may not appeal. Otherwise he may appeal as in Part 11, Rule 68.

PART 11—TOURNAMENT PLAY

63. For each tournament there shall be a tournament director selected who shall be empowered to: administrate, interpret and enforce The Rules of the Game; appoint a committee to assist and provide referees, timekeepers and deadness board attendants; arrange the draw; assign handicaps; schedule matches; assign courts and otherwise direct all aspects of the competition, including the disposition of any appeal by players or teams not resolved by the referee.

64. In tournaments, a time limit either per play and/or per game may be set by the tournament committee before the start of the first tournament game.

65. Until 15 minutes to the end of a time limit game (e.g. 2 hours or 1-1/2 hours), each player will be allowed no more than 75 seconds to begin his turn, following the completion of the opponent's last stroke. The timekeeper will announce the time remaining after one minute has elapsed and call 'TIME' at 75 seconds. If the player has not struck his ball (or waived), play immediately resumes with the next player.

66. When fifteen minutes remain in a game, the timekeeper shall so announce, and thereafter each player will be allowed no more than 45 seconds to begin his turn. During this final 15 minutes, each team is entitled to receive two (2) one minute time-out periods (in addition to the 45 seconds allowed). At one minute

remaining, the timekeeper shall turn his back to the court and announce 'TIME' when the minute has elapsed.

67. When 'TIME' is called, the player in play shall complete his turn (which is his last), and each remaining ball shall have one turn in rotation. The side which has cumulatively passed through the greatest number of wickets, including the stake, is declared the winner, but if there is now a tie, play shall continue in full rounds until the tie is broken or both balls of one side stake out.

68. If, during the course of a tournament, either the players or referee is unable to resolve a question of fact or law, they may appeal to the tournament director, who shall decide accordingly. If he by coincidence happens to have been a witness and is satisfied that he knows the answer, he should inform the players that he is deciding the subject matter of the appeal by observation, and give his decision accordingly.

If he is not so satisfied, he should decide the dispute by investigation. He should hear what the parties have to say. At his discretion he should hear witnesses. He should then give a decision to the best of his ability.

If he is in doubt he should, in the last resort, give a compromise decision, which may involve adjusting the clips arbitrarily and directing where the balls should be placed. This includes the right to decide that the players shall replay the disputed play or begin the game again.

CUSTOMS AND ETIQUETTE OF THE GAME

The following, while not including specific rules or penalty related action, should be considered important and helpful to the conduct and enjoyment of the game.

Presence on Court

A player should not remain on the court in line of sight or area of visibility while his adversary is playing, or move on to it until it is clear that he has finished or may be about to make a questionable stroke.

Expedition in Play

A player should play his strokes as quickly as possible, and in doubles should avoid wasting time in prolonged discussion with his partner. (More than 75 seconds is considered excessive.)

Spectators

Spectators should abstain from audible comments on the game; from offering advice to players during a game; and from calling attention to any error committed or about to be committed by any player. A spectator may reply to a question by a player on a point of fact with the consent of the adversary. A player should not take advantage of any error or omission unnoticed by himself or his partner to which his attention has been drawn during the game by the comments or attitude of spectators.

Advice and Aids

No player is entitled to advice from anyone other than his partner in doubles. It must be a matter of conscience how a player acts when in receipt of unsolicited information or advice. Warning a player other than a partner that he is about to run a wrong wicket or play with the wrong ball constitutes advice, and in tournaments players and spectators must not so warn.

A mark shall not be made, either inside or outside the court, for the purpose of guiding the striker in the direction or strength of a stroke. A partner may use his mallet to indicate a spot, but it must be removed before the stroke.

Questionable Stroke

A player about to play a stroke, of which either the fairness or the effect (i.e. possible foul or when aiming at a ball near a wicket) may be doubtful, should himself suggest to his adversary that a referee be called to watch the stroke.

When the Players' Opinions Differ

If a ball has to be replaced because of the carelessness of a player, the offending party should ordinarily defer to the opinion of the other. When the question is whether a roquet has been made on a ball or whether a ball has moved, the positive opinion is generally to be preferred to the negative opinion. If there are any reliable witnesses, the players should agree to consult them in order to solve differences; but no player should consult a witness without the expressed permission of the other player.

Testing the Position of a Ball

The striker should not test whether a ball has run a wicket by placing his mallet against the wicket without first consulting his opponent. Any such test should be made in conjunction with the opponent, or, if either party so desire, by a referee or independent person if available. The same principle applies when the question is whether a ball is out of bounds, or may be lifted, moved, or wiped, if the position of replacement is critical. All such decisions made between strokes should be made jointly.

When Calling a Referee

In tournaments, a referee should always be called before a questionable stroke, and all disputes should be referred to a referee. If the opponent fails to call a referee before what he should have recognized as a questionable stroke, he should not appeal. He should confine himself to requesting the striker to take the initiative in calling for a referee if another such stroke is about to be played. But it may be that the adversary is of the opinion that the striker is making faults such as "pushing" or "double tapping" in an unhampered stroke; if so, he should inform the striker with a view to a referee being called to watch a stroke.

RULE AMENDMENTS FOR
ADVANCED SIX-WICKET AMERICAN CROQUET

Rule 1 (Replaces Part I, Rule 2). It shall be counted as a fault if striker:

(a) In a single ball stroke pushes or pulls his ball.
NOTE: In above a "push" or a "pull" means maintaining contact between mallet and ball for an appreciable period or any acceleration following a check of the mallet head after its initial contact with the ball.

(b) Strikes his ball audibly or distinctly twice in the same stroke (double tap) or maintains contact between mallet and ball after his ball has hit another ball, except that no fault can be committed under this sub-law if the cause of the second hit or the maintenance of contact is due to the making of a roquet or to interference by a ball staked out in that stroke.

(c) Moves or shakes a ball at rest by hitting a wicket or stake with the mallet.

(d) Strikes his ball so as to cause it to touch an upright or the stake while still in contact with the mallet (crush stroke).

(e) Strikes his ball when lying in contact with an upright or the stake other than in a direction away from the upright or the stake (crush stroke), so the ball does not hit the wicket.

Penalty for Making a Fault

Unless the fault is condoned the striker's turn ends. No point can be scored and, except for a fault made during a croquet stroke wherein the striker's turn would have ended under Rule 51, the balls are replaced.

Rule 2 (Replaces Part 4, Rule 25). The croquet stroke and uses of extra strokes:

(a) After hitting a ball (roquet), the striker must place his ball in contact with the roqueted ball however he chooses (but it may not touch any other ball) and in the course of his next (croquet) stroke must move or shake that ball.
PENALTY: Unless the fault is condoned, the striker's turn ends with no credit being given for wicket or stake. His ball remains where it lies at the end of the stroke, and he is considered dead on that ball.

(b) After the croquet stroke, the striker shall be entitled to play an additional stroke unless his turn has ended under Rule 51 or has made another legal roquet, whereafter he would take croquet from that ball.
(Rules a and b above also replace Part 9, Rule 54).

144

(c)　The striker may not place his foot or hand on his ball during the croquet stroke.
(This rule also eliminates Part 9, Rule 53).

Rule 3　(Replaces Part 8, Rule 43). A rover's ball may only be driven into the stake (either by a roquet or croquet stroke) by another rover which is alive on it, whereupon it will be considered to have finished the game (and scored a point for itself), and shall be immediately removed from the court.

UNITED STATES CROQUET ASSOCIATION
OFFICIAL RULES
FOR THE NINE-WICKET GAME

On the following pages are the official rules for the nine-wicket, two stake croquet game as codified by the United States Croquet Association. Many of the rules are the same in both the nine-wicket game and the six-wicket game. To avoid unnecessary duplication, when the rules are the same, we have not spelled out the nine-wicket rule but, rather, have referred you back to the six-wicket section. When the nine-wicket rule is different, we spell out the variation in full.

Because the nine-wicket game is more wide open than the six-wicket game, you might want to use these rules as a guideline only and make exceptions as you see fit. The equipment, court conditions, and your own preferences should be the final arbitor.

INTRODUCTION TO
THE AMERICAN 9-WICKET 2-STAKE GAME

COURT LAYOUT AND SIZE VARIATIONS

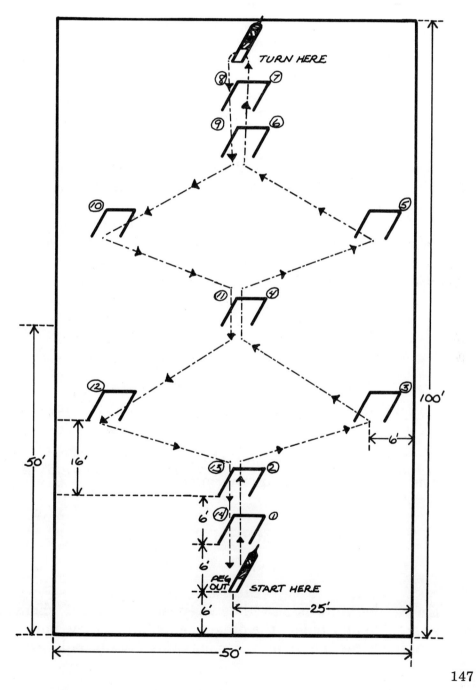

The Standard Court

The standard court is a rectangle, with the length two times the width (50' x 100' is recommended). Its boundaries shall be marked out clearly, the INSIDE edge of the definitive border being the actual boundary. (Nylon string or plastic tape stapled or otherwise affixed to the ground can be used for boundary lines.) The court may be scaled down proportionately, but smaller than 30' x 60' is not recommended.

The Standard Setting

Two stakes shall be set at each end of the court, 6 feet from the adjacent end's boundary line, and equidistant from each side of the boundary line. The first and seventh wickets shall be 12 feet from the adjacent end line and equidistant from each side-line. The 2nd and 6th wickets shall be 18 feet from the adjacent end-line and equidistant from the side-lines. The 4th wicket shall be set at the center of the court, equidistant from the side boundary lines. The four outside wickets (the 3rd, 5th, 7th and 9th) shall be set 34 feet from the adjacent end-line and 34 feet from the adjacent side boundary line.

The Wickets

The wickets are the same as in the six-wicket game, except they are all painted white.

The Stake, the Balls and the Mallets

The stake, the balls and the mallets remain the same as in the six-wicket game.

The Court Accessories

The court accessories are the same.

THE OBJECT OF THE GAME

Singles

The singles game is played between two players, of whom one plays the blue and black, the other the red and yellow balls. The object of the game is for a player to make both of his balls score the

14 wicket points and 2 stake points, a total of 32 points, before his adversary.

Doubles

The doubles game is played between two sides, each side consisting of two players. One team plays the blue and black balls and the other the red and yellow balls. Each player plays only one ball throughout the game. As in singles, the object is to have one team score the total of 32 points before their adversaries.

In Both Games

A ball scores a wicket by passing through the wicket in order and in the direction shown on the diagram. This is known as running a wicket. But a ball which has made a roquet cannot thereafter in the same stroke carom off that ball and score a point for itself. A ball which has scored all 14 wicket and the upper stake points is known as a rover. It can then score the stake point by hitting it.

How Play Is Made

Play is made by striking a ball with a mallet. For the essentials of fair stroke—see Part I of The Six Wicket Rules. The player so playing is called the striker, and the ball which he strikes, the striker's ball. The striker may never strike an adversary's ball. By striking his ball, the striker may cause any other ball to move and to score a point.

The Turn

The players play each turn in sequence (blue, red, black and yellow). A player is initially entitled to one stroke in a turn, after which his turn ends, unless in that stroke his striker's ball has scored a wicket or stake point, or hit another ball. When the wicket or upper stake is scored, the striker is entitled to play one continuation stroke. When another ball is hit, the striker is said to have made a roquet on that ball. He becomes 'dead' on that ball and is entitled to two extra strokes. The first of these two strokes is known as the croquet stroke, and is made after moving and placing the striker's ball in contact with or up to one mallet head away from the roqueted ball, which if in contact in the croquet stroke, is known as the croqueted ball. If, in the croquet stroke the croqueted ball is sent off the court, or the striker's ball is sent off the court without first having made another roquet, the turn ends. During a turn the striker may roquet each ball he is 'alive' on once, and he may make a further roquet on each ball provided that, since he has last roqueted it, his striker's ball has scored a wicket or upper stake point for itself and has thus cleaned itself of it's "deadness". Thus, by a series of strokes entitling him to continue, the striker may make one or more point, during one turn. Such a series is known as 'making a break'. But continuation strokes are not cumulative, so that a striker who:

(a) scores a wicket or upper stake and hits another ball in the same stroke may take one continuation stroke or roquet the ball and take two;

(b) makes a roquet in a croquet stroke, immediately takes croquet and continues accordingly;

(c) scores a wicket or upper stake for his striker's ball in a croquet stroke, plays only one continuation stroke;

(d) scores two wickets for his striker's ball in one stroke, plays only one continuation stroke.

Ball In Hand

A ball in hand is any ball which has to be moved, and is, therefore, lifted and given a fresh position on the court in accordance with the Rules i.e.:

(a) a ball which has made a roquet;

(b) a ball off the court;

(c) a ball which has to be re-positioned after a fault or irregularity.

Ball Off the Court

A ball off the court is a ball in hand as soon as it goes off the court or when its vertical axis crosses the boundary line (more than half-way over).

Replacement of Balls
Off the Court and Near Boundaries

After each stroke, all balls off the court shall be replaced one mallet head in from the point where they went out. At the end of each turn all balls within a mallet's head of the boundaries are replaced that length from the line.

Strategy

Along with the basic objective of scoring the 32 points first, each team or player (in singles) should employ those offensive or defensive moves which will restrict the progress of the opponents.

Clips should be placed on the top of the wicket for the first 7 wickets and on the side (upright) for the last 7 wickets.

This version should be played as diagrammed and the exceptions to the American Six Wicket rules are amended as noted below.

PREFACE RULES

1. The Start: Each player must place his ball on a pre-designated spot between the first wicket and the lower stake (usually three feet from the wicket). Upon striking the ball a player is in the game and is considered "alive" on all other balls in the game. Play progresses in rotation. Various clubs rule that a ball struck through the first or upper two wickets in one shot is entitled to two extra strokes. This is an optional local rule with the preferred rule being only one extra stroke for making both wickets.

2. Upper Stake Rule: The upper stake, when hit in proper order, rewards the player one extra stroke, removes any prior deadness, and counts as one point (i.e. is treated as having made a wicket).

3. Rover Rule: Only when a rover ball is caused to strike the final stake by a partner or its player, is that ball considered to have completed the game and is removed from the field (note: partner must also stake out for the team to win).

4. Should an opponent cause a rover ball to hit the final stake, the player so staked must remove his ball for his next two turns, and on his third turn (in rotation) must place his ball one mallet length or less from the final stake and hit up to the upper stake. In that shot, or subsequent turns, the player must hit the upper stake to return to the game as a rover (last deadness rule still stays in effect).

    (a) Only one rover may be staked out by the opponent at any one time. There is no limit on the number of times an opponent can stake out a rover ball.

(b) A rover staked out by an opponent is not in the game until hitting the upper stake and shall be treated as if he did not exist (i.e. no one can play off of or be played by him) until hitting that upper stake, at which point he receives one extra stroke.

With the above as basic rule differences, the following are direct rule references to be used with the STANDARD AMERICAN SIX-WICKET CROQUET RULES.

PART I—USE OF THE MALLET

These rules are consistent with those for the six-wicket game.

PART 2—STARTING THE GAME

6. The starting order of play is determined by a coin toss.
7. All balls must start from the starting-tee in the order shown on the stake (blue, red, black and yellow), and must continue in that order throughout the game, or until put out of play. Upon striking the ball a player is in the game and is considered "alive" on all other balls in the game. Play progresses in rotation. Various clubs rule that a ball struck through the first or upper two wickets in one shot is entitled to two extra strokes. This is an optional local rule, with the preferred rule being only one extra stroke awarded for making both wickets.
8. (and 9) These rules do not apply.
10. Rule 10 is the same, except a player is alive on all balls that have not made this wicket.
11. (12 and 13) These rules do not apply in 9-wicket croquet.

PART 3—MAKING A WICKET

Rules 14-20 are exactly the same.
21. On the placement of the clips, it should be noted that when running a wicket for the first time, the clip is placed on the crown and, when running the wicket in the opposite direction, the clip is attached to one of the uprights. This applies to the first seven wickets (in the nine-wicket game).

PART 4—ADDITIONAL STROKES

22. A player making a wicket in the correct sequence receives one additional stroke. In 9-wicket play, hitting the upper stake in

proper order rewards the player one extra stroke, removes any prior deadness, and counts as one point (i.e. is treated as having made a wicket).

23. The same.

24. A player who makes his wicket, or hits the upper stake and hits a ball on the same play, must hit that ball again to receive two extra strokes from it. He may, however, use his one additional stroke if he prefers, and shall not be considered "dead" on that ball. In both cases the ball roqueted is not replaced.

25. (and 26) The rules on the use of extra strokes are the same in both games.

PART 5—BISQUES

27. (to 32) concerning bisques and bisque use in handicap play are the same for both versions.

PART 6—DEAD BALL

33. (to 37) concerning "deadness" are the same for both versions.

PART 7—ALIVE BALL

38. (and 39) are the same in each. The ball is considered alive when it is driven through a wicket or against the upper stake.

PART 8—ROVER AND FINISHING THE GAME

40. A player who has made all the wickets and the upper stake is considered alive on all other balls.

43. Only when a rover ball is caused to strike the final stake by a partner or its player, is that ball considered to have completed the game and is removed from the field (note: partner must also stake out for the team to win).

44. Should an opponent cause a rover ball to hit the final stake, the player so staked must remove his ball for his next two turns and, on his third turn (in rotation), must place his ball one mallet length or less from the final stake and hit up to the upper stake. In that shot or subsequent turns, the player must hit the upper stake to return to the game as a rover (last deadness rule still stays in effect).

45. (through 48) Rules are the same for both 6- and 9-wicket croquet.

PART 9—FAULTS

48. (through 58) Rules are the same for both versions.

PART 10—REFEREES

59. (through 62) Rules dealing with referees and their duties are the same for each.

PART 11—TOURNAMENT PLAY

63. (through 68) The rules for tournaments apply to both the 6- and 9-wicket games.

Glossary

A-Class Player: A scratch player in American competition; In England, a player with a handicap of two or better.

Advanced Play (Laws of): The suggested rules of the United States Croquet Association.

Alive: In American play, a ball which has cleared a wicket but has not roqueted a ball is said to be alive. In the British game, all balls are alive at the start of every turn.

All-Round Break: Running all the hoops in a single turn.

American Roque League: Formed in 1916, it is the "Supreme Court" of roque, with chapters from coast to coast.

American System: The method of organizing a tournament that guarantees each player a number of games, by blocking them and having each play the others within his block.

Angle of Divergence: Angle at which balls part when a croquet shot is made.

Angle of Split: On a croquet shot, the angle between two lines, along which the two balls travel.

Association Croquet: Synonymous with British rules as played throughout the Commonwealth. The Santa Barbara club is the only American member of England's Croquet Association.

Aunt Emma: A conservative player who wastes his or her talent through dull and uninspired play.

Back Peel: Peeling a ball through its own hoop, immediately after you have run that hoop.

Baire: A game played in 7th century Ireland; possibly a primitive form of croquet.

Ball In Hand: A ball that has to be picked up and moved, either before taking croquet or because it has gone out-of-bounds.

Basket: Crossed center wickets once used in garden croquet. It also refers to the area of the center arches in roque.

Baulk-Line: On each of the short sides of the yard-line are other unmarked lines, approximately twelve yards in length, known as the baulk-lines. In British play, these are, in effect, the starting lines.

B-Class Player: A +2 handicap player in America; in England, one with a handicap of between 2-1/2 and 6.

Beefy Shot: A long, hard shot.

Being Off Color: The opposite of hitting true.

Beugelspel: A Dutch game that is similar to croquet and its forerunner pall mall.

Big Handicap: An all-comer's event, usually held during British club tournaments.

Bisque: A unit of difference between two player's handicaps, it is the number of extra turns given to the player with the highest handicap.

Bisque Extraction: Strategy of making your opponent use up his bisques ineffectively or for defensive purposes only.

Bombard: The croquet shot in roque.

Break: The method of extending your turn by using one or more of the other balls.

Break Down: To err so that your turn involuntarily comes to an end during the course of a break.

British Open Championship: British singles title, played annually at Roehamp-hampton.

Cage: Another name for crossed wickets, an arrangement used in garden croquet.

Camanachd: Scotch Gaelic for hurley, a game similar to baire and hockey.

Cannon Shot: To make a roquet on the same stroke as a croquet shot, that is, to make a croqueted ball hit another.

Carrying Through: Following through with your arms leading; term coined by Lord Tollemache.

C-Class Player: A player with a handicap of greater than six (in England), or greater than two in the United States.

Center Style: Traditional stance with mallet between-the-knees.

Cleaning Yourself: Becoming "undead" by running a hoop or, in England, becoming alive at the end of your turn.

Clips: The color of each ball, these are placed on the hoops to mark the player's progress.

Cluiche: The Irish word for play; it is pronounced "crooky."

Cold Ball: The roque, the last played ball of your opponent.

Condoning: Failure of a player to claim a foul within the limit of claims makes the play in question valid, with no foul charged to the striker.

Consignificant Crouching: An archaic etymological form of "croquet."

Contact: To touch or make contact with another ball.

Continuation Stroke: The extra stroke earned by running a hoop; also earned when a roquet is made, it is used after first taking croquet.

Corner: To hit your ball into a corner for defensive purposes.

Corner Balls: Balls sent off the court that are returned to a point within one yard of a corner (English).

Corner Cannon Shot: Combination of rush and croquet stroke; you roquet a ball after taking croquet from another ball that is in the corner.

Corner Flags: Placed at the four corners of the course; seldom used in the United States.

Corner Pegs: These are placed a yard on each side of each flag.

Count Upon: In roque, you are said to count upon another ball when you make contact with it.

Coupe Croquet: A parlor game which combines billiards and marbles.

Crochet: An old French dialect form of "croquet."

Crooky: An old Irish game, claimed by some to be a forerunner of croquet.

Croquet Association: Founded as the All England Croquet Club, it is now the world's governing body (with the exception of the United States).

Croquet Carnival: Tournaments held annually by the Australian Croquet Association. Among the events are the Interstate Cup Competition and the English Medal Event.

Croquet Golf (Golf Croquet): A variation of croquet in which the hoops are treated as if they were holes in golf.

Croquet Shot: Sometimes called a drive shot, the stroke you earn after making a roquet. Your ball is placed against the roqueted ball, and in taking croquet, you send both your own and your opponent's ball to desired positions. In American rules a croquet shot can be taken a mallet-head's length away from the object ball.

Cross Peg: A leave in which the enemy balls are left straddling the peg, thus preventing or impeding your foe's intended shot.

Cross Wire: A leave in which the enemy balls are left on each side of a hoop, thus preventing your foe from taking his desired shot.

Crown: The top part of a hoop (the crossbar).

Crush Shot: Used to jar a ball through its hoop, when the ball is laying against the hoop; it is legal only in the American game.

Cuppers Competition: An elimination competition among British college teams.

Cut Rush: A shot played so that the rushed ball moves off at an angle to the direction of the stroke.

Deadness Board: Implement used to keep track of who is dead on which ball.

Deadness: When you hit another ball with your own, you can no longer use that ball for the duration of your turn (except for the croquet shot), until running a hoop in the American game, or for British play, until the end of your turn.

Delayed Triple Peel: Abandoning a triple peel temporarily, to be resumed later in your turn.

Destroy Shot: A shot hit with unusual force in order to send a croqueted ball the largest distance possible; an American term.

Double Banking: Playing two games on the same lawn simultaneously, due to space or time shortage; the games are completely separate.

Double Elimination: Type of tournament in which a player must lose two matches before being eliminated.

Double Peel: A ball knocked through two hoops in the same turn, but not necessarily on two successive strokes.

Double Roll: A shot in which the striker's ball travels the same distance as the croqueted ball.

Double Tap: A fault in which the striker's ball is hit twice during the same swing.

Double Target: Two balls so placed, or a ball and a hoop so grouped, that the effective target area is doubled.

Draw: One of the two competition cards used in the two-life system of determining the matches in a tournament event.

Drive Shot: By hitting very slightly down on your ball during a croquet shot, your foe's ball will go roughly three times farther than your own.

English Medal Event: A part of the Croquet Carnival in which ten players from each Australian state compete for medals donated by the Croquet Association of England.

Fair Position: In roque, a ball that has properly cleared its hoop is said to be in fair position.

Fault: An unacceptable, or foul stroke.

Feather-Off: A light take-off shot.

Foot Shot: A croquet shot taken with your foot on your ball; it is legal only in American standard play.

Forestalling: If you foul and your opponent does not stop play before your next stroke to claim a misplay, no penalty is assessed, and the foul is said to be forestalled.

Four-Ball Break: The backbone of the game, a play in which all four balls are used to maneuver your way around the court, ideally in a single turn.

Free Shot: A shot which, if missed, will not immediately have any dangerous consequences.

Full-Bisque Play: A variety of handicap play in which the players are allowed to use all of their respective bisques, as opposed to the standard system which allows only the inferior player to use bisques.

Garden Croquet: Amateur, unofficial, backyard croquet; the most popular and well-known variety of the sport. Usually played with nine wickets and two stakes.

Golf Style: Style of swinging in which the mallet is swung across the body like a putter.

Go To Bed With Bisques: To lose in a handicap game with one or more unused bisques.

Hale Setting: Introduced in 1872, a court arrangement with six hoops and two pegs; replaced by the Willis Setting.

Half-Bisque: An extra shot used in handicap doubles and some singles, in which you cannot score points; hence they are used for maneuvering the ball. British.

Half-Jump Shot: By hitting down on the ball, you try to drive both your ball and the obstructing ball through the hoop.

Hidden Ball: A roque term, this is a ball that cannot be hit by the enemy without a foul stroke or bank shot, due to its position on the court.

Hitting True: Hitting the ball with a level swing, as opposed to hitting up or down.

157

Holden, 'Doc' Milton Trophy: Awarded to Eastern Seaboard Singles Champion.

Home Run: In roque, when a ball scores all of its points in a single turn, it has made a home run.

Hong Kong: Archaic term for taking croquet.

Hoop-Bound: When one's swing is impeded by a hoop.

Hoop-Running Shot: A shot through your proper hoop.

Hot Ball: In roque, foe's next played ball.

Hurlingham Club: London club, site of the British Open Championship and the Croquet Association.

Innings: When the balls are arranged so that you are more likely to score points than your opponent, you are said to be "in," and thus have the innings. In roque, an inning is a full turn by all the players.

Interstate Cup: Known also as the Eire Cup, the object of an annual competition held between the six states of Australia.

Irish Grip: A grip with the palms of both hands held away from the body; it originated with the great Irish players of the Edwardian Era.

Irish Peel: A roll stroke which is similar to a half-jump shot, in that both balls go through their wickets.

Irish Style: Similar to the center style, but using the Irish grip.

Is For: The next hoop that a ball must run, e.g. "yellow is for third hoop."

Jam: An illegal shot made with unlawfully prolonged contact between the ball and the arch when a ball lies against a hoop; similar to a carry in volleyball.

Jaws: Entrance to the uprights of a hoop.

Join Up: To play your ball to a spot near its partner ball.

Jump Ball: By hitting down on your ball, you can make it jump over an obstructing ball; it is prohibited on some courses.

King Ball: Ball in royal roque that supercedes the rover ball.

Kiss Cannon: Like a corner cannon shot except for the added element of hitting a third ball with the croqueted ball, as well as roqueting your intended target with your own ball.

Knock-Out: An elimination system in tournaments in which a single loss means elimination.

Knocking-Up: Hitting practice balls to get the lie of a course.

Lag: Method of determining the right of choice in roque and garden croquet; like the one used in pool.

Lay Up: A long, wild or reckless shot; made to escape from a dangerous position or to waste a shot when you are uncertain as to your next move.

Laying a Break: Positioning balls at future hoops to set up a possible break.

Level Play: Non-handicap competition.

Lift: Any situation that calls for picking up a ball, as in prior to taking croquet, or when a ball is driven out of bounds.

Limit of Claims: Time during which a fault can be called, or else it is invalid.

Long Bisquer: Player with a high handicap.

Longman Cup: Trophy given annually since 1926 to winners of the handicap competition among croquet clubs in England.

Lower Stake: The near stake in the American nine-wicket layout, and the eighth and sixteenth points in a roque course.

Macrobertson International Shield: International competition held every four years since 1925; involves England (with the most wins), New Zealand, and Australia.

McGowan Trophy: An award given by the American Roque League.

Moreton-In-The-Marsh: A town in Western England which was the site of the first all-comers' tournament.

National Croquet Association: American group formed in 1882, at the nadir of croquet's popularity, it helped spark new interest in the sport. Now defunct.

National Regulation Croquet: An American game which is a combination of croquet and roque, and is played on a roque court.

Net Points: The total number of points scored minus the total number of points scored against; they are used to break ties under the American System in Britain, if the number of games won are tied.

Next-Two Leave: A leave whereby you leave your partner with a rush to his hoop and one enemy ball at each of the next two hoops for your future use.

No Brainer: A lucky shot.

Non-Playing Side: Area behind a hoop as you approach that wicket from the proper direction.

Norwich, Connecticut: Entry point of croquet from Europe into the United States, it was the site of rule revisions in 1899.

Off The . . . : When you score a hoop off a certain ball, you are said to have made it, for example, "off the red."

Official Handicap Book: Contains handicaps of all players registered with England's Croquet Association.

Official Regulation Croquet: American game which is a combination of roque and croquet. Sanctioned by the American Roque League; it should not be confused with lawn croquet as played under U.S.C.A. rules.

One-Ball Shot: A shot in which only one ball is hit.

Out Player: The player who does not have the innings.

Pall Mall: An early version of croquet that was a favorite of Charles II; also spelled *paille maille* and *pesle mesle*.

Pass Roll: A croquet shot in which you send your ball farther than the croqueted ball.

Peel: Causing a ball other than your own to run its proper hoop.

Peg Down: To interrupt a game, marking the position of the balls and clips, with the intention of resuming later.

Pegged-Out Game: Game in which at least one ball has been pegged-out.

Penultimate: The next-to-last hoop.

Pig Pen: The crossed center wickets occasionally used in nine-wicket croquet. Also known as "the basket."

Pilot Ball: The ball off which you make a hoop in a four-ball break.

Pioneer Ball: In a three- or four-ball break, the ball that is sent forward to the hoop after the one you are going for.

Pivot Ball: The middle ball in a four-ball break; it is placed near the peg on the side you are then playing.

Playing Line: A line on a roque court that corresponds to the yardline on a British course.

Playing Side: Area in front of a hoop as your ball approaches it.

Plaza-Toro Technique: Miller and Thorp's term for letting yourself be carried by your mallet instead of carrying through with your arms leading; named for the Duke of Plaza-Toro, who liked to lead his regiment from behind.

Predominance: A common error in which one hand or foot leads your swing too much.

President's Cup: Major British tournament for the United Kingdom's best eight players; played with a 1/16th inch clearance of ball through hoop, instead of the usual 1/8th inch.

Process: Along with the draw, one of two competition cards used in determining the line-up and seeding for tournament events.

Pseudo-Cannon Shot: A three-ball croquet shot in which you move the croqueted ball just a little way out of the corner.

Pull: The tendency in a croquet shot for the balls to curve in an inward manner from their line of aim.

Push: Keeping the mallet on the ball for an appreciable time after hitting it; it is allowed only on a croquet shot—so long as your mallet does not speed up when in contact with the ball.

Quadruple Peel: A four-wicket peel.

Qualifying Shot: The shot which begins your turn.

Queen Ball: The neutral ball in royal roque.

Questionable Stroke: A play of dubious legality, or in which there is a great chance of a foul; on such a controversial play, the contestants should consult the referee before the shot is made.

Quintuple Peel: A rarely seen five-wicket peel.

Referee on Appeal: An English term for requesting the referee to rule on a controversy after the act has occurred.

Referee on Call: On some plays, such as a questionable stroke, the referee should be requested to act on the controversy before the play in question occurs; also an English term.

Reverse Palm Grip: The most popular grip, it is made with the lower hand's palm away from the body and the upper hand's knuckles away from the body.

Right of Choice: After a lag or a toss of a coin, the winner has the option of choosing starting position or choice of balls.

Rigor Mortis: Being dead on all balls, and therefore unable to move with the assistance of the other balls for the duration of your turn; also known as three ball dead or three B D.

Roehampton: One of England's most famous croquet clubs, it is the home of the Roehampton Rovers and the Roehampton League.

Roehampton League: The Roehampton team challenges other clubs in this competition, and this, as well as the growth of English university teams has helped the expansion of inter-club competition in the United Kingdom.

Roehampton Rovers: The Roehampton Club's team in the league named after it.

Roll Stroke: A croquet shot used to add distance to the flight of your own ball as well as the croqueted ball, it is taken with a downward sweep instead of a level swing.

Roque News Two-Ball Trophy: Given to roque's national two-ball champion.

Roquet: When a ball is hit and made to hit another ball (either deliberately or by accident); it is generally followed by a croquet shot and continuation stroke.

Rover Ball: One that has passed through all the hoops but has not yet hit the final peg; it can make moves on all other balls in a given turn, as deadness does not apply to the rover.

Rover Hoop: The last hoop before the final peg.

Routledge's Handbook of Croquet: English publication written by Edmund Routledge in 1861, it is probably the first rule book of the game, and with numerous modifications, basically still governs croquet.

Royal Roque: A variation of roque which features a neutral white ball, called the queen ball, and a king ball, which supercedes a rover ball.

Rush (Long or Short): A roquet shot which sends the roqueted ball in a given direction.

Rush Line: An imaginary line along which a ball is roqueted on a rush shot.

Rush Line Principle: The shot made before an intended rush shot should be taken from a spot on or near the rush line.

Scatter: A shot played only as a last resort which separates balls that lie too close together.

Schedule of Bisques: The number of bisques awarded according to the type of event.

Scratch Player: As in golf, a croquet player with a handicap of zero.

Sextuple Peel: Part of a plan to finish the game in two breaks; similar to a quadruple peel, just extended. J.W. Solomon is renowned for making two successful sextuple peels to win an Open championship.

Shepherding: Illegal ploy of letting your mallet guide your ball through the hoop by a push rather than by a legal stroke.

Side: Technique in which the ball is not struck with the center of your mallet; used for cut rushes or for making awkward wickets.

Split Shot: A croquet shot in which both balls go off at different angles.

Split: A roque term for making contact with a ball and causing it to move; in roque, shots that are not splits are direct shots.

Spread Wickets: A garden arrangement whereby you separate certain wickets for added difficulty.

Stalk: Walking up behind a ball in the line you wish to send it, in order to insure proper aim.

Stepping Stone: When your ball is placed near a hoop or the peg, in a position that is advantageous to your partner.

Sticky Wicket: Having a difficult approach to a hoop, or being stuck in a hoop; also the name of a bi-annual croquet tournament held in Centre Isle, Oyster Bay, N.Y.

Stop Shot: By delivering an upward blow to one's own ball on a croquet shot, you drive the croqueted ball a considerable distance, while your ball barely moves.

Straight Croquet: A shot in which the striker's ball goes half the distance of the croqueted ball.

Straight Triple Peel: Doing three peels with the backward ball making the same three hoops.

Striker: Player whose turn it is.

Stroke: Any movement of the mallet that deliberately or otherwise results in movement of the ball.

Stymie: A ball blocking the intended path of your own ball.

Surrey Cup: A championship held at Cheltenham in the same week in September as the President's Cup Tourney, for the next best eight United Kingdom players (behind those who competed for the President's Cup).

Take-Off Shot: A croquet shot in which the croqueted ball moves a little, but the striker's ball moves a great distance.

Thick Take-Off: A croquet shot in which the croqueted ball moves a somewhat greater distance than on a simple take-off, and the striker's ball goes a considerable distance.

Three-Ball Break: Break using three balls, it is the corner-stone of the pegged-out game.

Tice: A shot which places your ball in a position where your foe is likely to shoot at it, but your ball is a sufficient distance from your foe that he is likely to miss should he attempt it.

Two-Ball Break: Break using two balls, it is the most difficult of all the breaks, as it involves shots of the greatest distance.

Two-Life System: Method of setting up competition in a tournament, using draw and process cards, it has the asset of mixing byes and matches throughout the card.

Upright Style: Another name for the front style of swinging your mallet outside your feet, which gives you greater freedom of movement and additional power.

Up the Country: Another name for taking croquet.

Victoria Park Electric Light Carnival: Sponsored by the Western Australian Croquet Association, it features croquet played every night from January 28 to February 22.

Waive: To pass your turn.

Wall Shot: In roque a shot used in which you carom your ball off the surrounding wall when you are unable to make a direct shot on your intended target.

Widow Ball: In roque, a three-ball variety with a neutral ball called the widow ball.

Willis Setting: Introduced in 1922, it is the present-day court arrangement using one center peg and six hoops.

Winter Wickets: Thin wickets used when the ground is hard or frozen.

Wired Ball: A ball behind a wicket or peg that cannot be hit by the striker's ball or other ball because of the obstruction.

Yard-Line Area: On an English court, an unmarked area surrounding the playing field which includes two baulk-lines.

Yard-Line Ball: In British play, a ball that is sent out of bounds and is replaced on the yard-line at a point where it left the court.

Yousey Trophy: A trophy competed for in roque.

G. Nigel Aspinall

Records and Rosters

ROSTER OF CROQUET PLAYERS

Arnold, Bobby: Seven-time American roque champion.

Aspinall, G. Nigel: One of the top world players presently competing. A Briton, he currently holds the only -5 handicap. Aspinall is the current British Open Champion and winner of the President's cup.

Beaton, R.C.J.: Two-time winner of British Open Title and four-time mixed doubles winner. An outstanding United Kingdom player of the 1920's and 1930's.

Bray, Roger: One of the better players currently competing, this Englishman once held a -5 handicap.

Clark, Ed: Six-time American roque champion, he won his last two titles thirteen years apart. From Springfield, Massachusetts.

Corbally, Cyril: A great Irish player, he introduced new skills and tactics into croquet, aiding in the game's resurgence from 1890 to World War I.

Cotter, E.P.C.: Outstanding British player and author, frequent doubles partner of J.W. Solomon.

Crane, Mrs. V.C.: Current Australian champion, from Victoria.

Crosby, Samuel: Helped form the American Roque League, and is responsible for coining the word "roque."

Drummond, Capt.: Founded England's Croquet Association with Walter Peel.

Duke of Marlborough: Formerly the unofficial social leader of the Southampton, Long Island, N.Y. croquet set.

Dupre, Lt. Col. W.B.: Outstanding United Kingdom croquet player of the 1920's and 1930's; frequent doubles partner of D.D. Steel.

Elvey, Rev. G.F. Handel: Croquet author, he was president of England's croquet Association in the 1940's and 1950's.

Goldwyn, Samuel: Famed Hollywood producer and croquet aficionado, he installed a sand-trap on his home course to thwart the likes of Louis Jourdan and Darryl F. Zanuck.

Green, Jack: From Long Beach, California, he has won five titles in two-ball roque.

Hicks, Humphrey O.: Five-time British Open winner since 1932, he was the holder of the lowest handicap ever, -5½; he plays with an unorthodox side-style.

Jacobus, Charles: Winner of roque competition at 1904 Olympics in St. Louis, he is the sport's only Olympic champion.

Jacques, John: An enterprising young Frenchman, he was probably the first to manufacture croquet equipment. The company he established is now the world's oldest sporting goods manufacturer.

Joad, Mrs.: First winner of the Women's Championship for croquet in England, in 1869.

Jourdan, Louis: Perhaps the most talented croquet player among the celebrity set.

Marx, Harpo: Along with the Algonquin Set he helped popularize croquet in the United States in the 1920's through 1940's.

Matthews, P.D. "Duff": Along with Leslie O'Callaghan and Cyril Corbally, one of the great Irish players who helped revitalize the game before World War I.

Mitsch, Rex: From Glendale, California, he holds five titles in two-ball roque.

O'Callaghan, Leslie: One of the triumvirate of great Irish players before the first World War.

Oddie, Miss N.: Frequent mixed doubles partner of John Solomon, 1954 English mixed doubles winner.

Ormerod, Dr. W.: 1975 doubles winner with G. Nigel Aspinall, once held a -5 handicap. Author of a croquet book and present head of the British Croquet Association.

Osborn, Jack: Founder, Executive Director of the United States Croquet Association, he is a top-ranked American player over the last fifteen years of competition. President of the N.Y.C.C.

Peck, Archie: A highly-ranked American player. President, Palm Beach Croquet Club. Director of U.S.C.A.

Peel, Walter: Early champion (1868) who founded England's Croquet Association with Captain Drummond.

Prentis, Ted: One of the top American players; former Eastern U.S. Singles title-ist, a member of the Westhampton Mallet Club and New York Croquet Club; Director U.S.C.A.

Reckitt, Geoffrey: One of the great British players and authorities on croquet.

Reid, Captain Mayne A.: American boys' author and Mexican War hero who helped popularize croquet with his 1863 book.

Robertson, Sir MacPherson: Donated MacRobertson Shield in 1925 to the Croquet Association for international test matches held every four to six years between England, Australia and New Zealand.

Ross, Arthur G.: A New Zealander, he is an eleven-time New Zealand champion and respected authority on the game.

Routledge, Edmund: Author of Routledge's Handbook on Croquet, probably the game's first rule book.

Rounds, W.A.: First president of the American Roque League, he also incorporated that group.

Shipman, A.G.: The first American croquet champion in 1882; from New York City.

Solomon, John W.: The "Babe Ruth" of croquet, with more than fifty titles to his credit; presently holds a handicap of -4; has the most international appearances and the most wins in international competition.

Steel, D.D.: Fifteen-time womens' champion, four-time British Open champion and holder of seven mixed doubles titles, she was perhaps the foremost woman player in the history of the sport.

Stephens, Wayne: Seven-time American roque champion.

Strachan, Douglas: Irish champion during the 1960's, he is a member of England's Hurlingham Club.

Swope, Herbert Jr.: One of the top-rated American players, his father helped popularize croquet in this country as part of the Algonquin Set. Co-founder and former president N.Y.C.C. and Director U.S.C.A.

Tankoos, S. Joseph: One of the better American players, he is the chairman of the New York Croquet Club and Director U.S.C.A.

Tollemache, Baron John Lyonel: A famous English croquet player and author, his book is possibly the longest on the subject of croquet.

Whitmore, Walter-Jones: Winner of the first British Open championship, he invented new rules for the game (both of which declined in popularity). He was the first to attempt a codification of rules and devise a system of tactics for croquet.

Windsor, M.S.: A great Australian champion, with five appearances in MacRobertson Shield Competition, he is now a manufacturer of high-level croquet equipment.

Woollcott, Alexander: A major croquet advocate, the author, playwright and raconteur had his own course on Neshobe Island in Vermont.

Wylie, Keith: A top player, he used champagne corks to lighten his mallets.

Zanuck, Darryl F.: Hollywood producer who is one of the game's great devotees, he has his own elaborate course in Palm Springs.

UNITED STATES
CROQUET ASSOCIATION
RANKINGS FOR MEN

(As of Spring, 1976 Eastern Singles)

1. Archie Peck.
2. Jack R. Osborn.
3. Dick Pearman.*
4. Ted Prentis.
5. John Young Jr.
6. Herbert Bayard Swope Jr.
7. S. Joseph Tankoos.
8. Andrew Fuller.**
9. E.A. Prentis III.
10. Alfred Heath.
11. Ed Howe.
12. Hal Finsness.
13. Arthur Bohner.
14. Vincent C. Ross Jr.
15. Walter P. Margulies.
16. Bill Bohner.
17. Louis Gourd.
18. Henry White.
19. Malcolm Martin.
20. David Seiniger.
21. Bayfield Clark.

  * Did not compete in 1976 Singles (1975 Defending Champion).
 ** Did not compete in 1976 Singles.

LATEST UNITED STATES
CROQUET ASSOCIATION
RANKINGS FOR WOMEN

(As of January, 1976)

1. Nelga Young.
2. Josie Finsness.
3. Hilda McMartin.
4. Sarah Churchill Roubanis.
5. Kitty Martin.
6. Sarah Doyle.
7. Valarie Heath.
8. Ginny Coulter.
9. Cathy Tankoos.
10. Betty Prentis.
11. Harriet Margulies.
12. Lee Messmore.
13. Barton Gubelman.
14. Gete Pasley.
15. Kit Liberman.
16. Ellie Griggs.
17. Kate Jennings.
18. Alice Gates.
19. Irene Charles.
20. Sandy Seininger.

BRITISH CROQUET ASSOCIATION TOP 20 PLAYERS AS OF 1975

TOP 8 (1975 President's Cup) In order of finish.

1. G. Nigel Aspinall.
2. A.B. Hope.
3. Prof. B.G. Neal.
4. M.E.W. Heap.
5. J.W. Solomon.
6. P.J. Bulloch.
7. S.R. Hemsted.
8. G.E.P. Jackson.

Unavailable to play in 1976 President's Cup, but top-ranked.

9. William Pritchard.

10. William Ormerod.
11. Keith Wylie.
12. Paul Hands.

Chairman's Salver (Second best 8 in order of finish).

13. C.H.L. Pritchard.
14. D.V.H. Rees.
15. W.R. Bulloch.
16. R.A. Godby.
17. A.V. Camroux.
18. Mrs. D.M.C. Pritchard.
19. J.A. Wheeler.
20. Mrs. K.M.O. Wheeler.

NEW ZEALAND PLAYER RANKINGS AS OF 1974 TEST MATCHES

		Wins vs. # of games played.
1.	J.G. Prince.	9/12.
2.	G.D. Rowling.	6/12.
3.	A.M. Anderson.	6/12.
4.	R.V. Jackson.	5/12.
5.	C.E. Anderson.	3/12.
6.	R.J. Murfit.	3/12.

AUSTRALIAN PLAYER RANKINGS AS OF 1974 TEST MATCHES

		Wins vs. # of games played.
7.	S.A. Buck.	6/12.
8.	R.J. Magor.	4/12.
9.	A.B. Russell.	4/12.
10.	H.J. Read.	3/12.
11.	B.M. Chambers.	3/12.
12.	N.E. Spooner.	3/8.
13.	Mrs. R. Chapman.	0/4.

RESULTS OF COMPETITION FOR THE MAC-ROBERTSON INTERNATIONAL SHIELD (1925-1974)

YEAR	HELD IN	RESULT
1925	England	England 3 Australia 0
1927	Australia	Australia 1 England 1 (Australia won on the basis of total games)
1930	Australia	Australia 3 New Zealand 0
1935	Australia	Australia 4 England 3 New Zealand 0 (Australia and England each with two ties)
1937	England	England 5 Australia 0
1950	New Zealand	New Zealand 2 England 1
1956	England	England 5 New Zealand 0
1963	New Zealand	England 6 Australia 2 New Zealand 1

There was no further competition until 1969, when England won for a record fourth time. In 1974, England retained the trophy by defeating New Zealand and third-place Australia. 1979 will mark the next competition, in games held in New Zealand. International play was suspended during the war years.

NATIONAL TWO-BALL ROQUE CHAMPIONS

Player	Home	Where Held	Date
Robert Arnold	Los Angeles	Dallas	1958
Emmitt Gladish	Los Angeles	Long Beach	1959
Robert Arnold	Los Angeles	Decatur, Ill.	1960
Arm Kapigian	La Canada, Cal.	Santa Monica	1961
Harry Rosenberg	San Diego	San Diego	1962
Arm Kapigian	La Canada, Cal.	Glendale, Cal.	1963
Robert Arnold	El Monte, Cal.	Los Angeles	1964
Rex Mitsch	Glendale, Cal.	Glendale	1965
Jack Green	Long Beach	Glendale	1966
Rex Mitsch	Glendale	Santa Monica	1967

Jack Green	Long Beach	Glendale	1968
Jack Green	Long Beach	Bixby Park, Cal.	1969
Rex Mitsch	Glendale	Long Beach	1970
Rex Mitsch	Glendale	Bixby Park, Cal.	1971
Jack Green	Long Beach	Long Beach	1972
Jack Green	Long Beach	Bixby Park, Cal.	1973
Rex Mitsch	Sepulveda, Cal.	Long Beach	1974

Records of G. Nigel Aspinall

President's Cup Champion: 1969, 1970, 1974, 1975.

British Open Singles Champion: 1969, 1974, 1975.

British Open Singles Runner-Up: 1968, 1970, 1971.

British Open Doubles Champion: 1966, 1968, 1970, 1971, 1972, 1975.

National Handicap Winner: 1972.

MacRobertson Shield Team Member: 1969, 1974.

Records of John William Solomon

10 titles in the Open Croquet Championship:
1953, 1956, 1959, 1961, 1963 through 1968.

10 titles in the Mens' Championship:
1951, 1953, 1958 through 1960, 1962, 1964, 1965, 1971 and 1972.

10 titles in the Doubles Open Event (with E.P.C. Cotter):
1954, 1955, 1958, 1959, 1961 through 1965, and 1969.

9 titles in the President's Silver Cup Event:
1955, 1957 through 1959, 1962 through 1964, and 1968 through 1971.

4 titles in the Champion of Champions Event (winning all four times this event has been run):
1967, 1968, 1969 and 1970.

2 titles in the New Zealand Open:
1951 and 1963.

2 titles in the New Zealand Open Doubles Championship:
1951 (with H.O. Hicks) and 1963 (with E.P.C. Cotter).

1 title in Mixed Doubles (with Miss N. Oddie):
1954.

1 title in Open Doubles of Australia (with H.O. Hicks):
1951.

MISCELLANEOUS 1974 RESULTS

Eastern Seaboard Singles Championship "Doc Holden Trophy."
Held March 15-17 at Palm Beach, Florida.
Winner: Archie Peck, Palm Beach.
Runner-Up: Andy Fuller, Palm Beach.

Palm Beach Invitational:
Held January 25-27 at Palm Beach, Florida.
Winners: Jack Osborn, New York and Lady Sarah Churchill Roubanis, Greece.
Runners-Up: Archie Peck, Palm Beach and Dick Pearman, Bermuda.

New York Croquet Club Tournament:
Held May 10-12 in New York, N.Y.
Winners: Ted Prentis and Joe Tankoos, both of New York.
Runners-Up: Andy Fuller, Palm Beach and Theo Roubanis, Greece.

New York Croquet Club Singles:
Held in October in New York, N.Y.
Winner: Ted Prentis, New York.
Runner-Up: Jack Osborn, New York.

New York Croquet Club Fall Invitational:
Held October 11-13 in New York, N.Y.
Winners: Joe Tankoos and Robert Liberman, of New York.

Runners-Up: Hilda McMartin, Bermuda and Allan Murray, Southampton, N.Y.

British Open Championship:
Final Round, Best of three games.
Singles: G.N. Aspinall beat A.M. Anderson, plus 5 and plus 23.
Doubles: J.G. Prince and G.D. Rowling beat A.B. Hope and M. Murray, minus 17, plus 12 and plus 16.

President's Cup:
Held in September at Hurlingham Club, London.
Winner: N.G. Aspinall.
Runner-Up: J.W. Solomon.

Australian Championship:
Singles: Mrs. V.C. Crane, Victoria.
Runner-Up: Mr. T.W. Howat, Victoria.

Women's: Mrs. V.C. Crane, Victoria.
Runner-Up: Mrs. S. MacDonald, West Australia.

Men's: Mr. T.W. Howat, Victoria.
Runner-Up: Mr. L. Moebus, Victoria.
Doubles: Mrs. L. Bray and Mr. W. Wilson, Queensland.
Runners-Up: Mr. and Mrs. T.W. Howat, Victoria.

MISCELLANEOUS 1975 RESULTS

Palm Beach Invitational:
Held January 24-26 at Palm Beach, Florida.
Winners: John Young II and Hilda McMartin, both of Bermuda.

Eastern Seaboard Singles "Doc Holden Trophy:"
Held March 14-16 at Palm Beach, Florida.
Winner: Dick Pearman, Bermuda.

Bellows' Cup Doubles Team Championship:
Held March 14-16 at Palm Beach, Florida.
Winner: Bermuda.
Runner-Up: New York Croquet Club.

Bermuda Croquet Club Invitational:
Held May 9-11, Bermuda.
Winners: John Young II and Hilda McMartin, both of Bermuda.
Runners-Up: Jack Osborn, New York and Kitty Martin, Bermuda.

New York Croquet Club Tournament:
Held May 30-June 1, New York, N.Y.
Winners: Jack Osborn, New York and Nelga Young, Bermuda.
Runners-Up: Ted Prentis, New York and Duncan McMartin, Bermuda.

Bi-Annual Oyster Bay Sticky Wicket Invitational:
Held September 26-28, Centre Isle, Long Island.
Winners: Jack Osborn and Cathy Tankoos, New York.
Runners-Up: Ted Prentis and Barton Gubelman, New York.

New York Croquet Club Fall Invitational:
Held October 10-12, New York, N.Y.
Winners: Ted Prentis and Cathy Tankoos, New York.
Runners-Up: Herbert Swope, Jr. and Henry S. White, New York.

British Open Championships:
Held July 14-19 at Hurlingham in London.
Singles Winner: G. Nigel Aspinall (plus 26 and plus 26).
Singles Runner-Up: T. Barlow.
Doubles Winners: G. Nigel Aspinall and Dr. W.P. Ormerod (plus 13 and plus 5).
Doubles Runners-Up: K.A. Ross and M.E.W. Heap.

President's Cup:
Held in September at Hurlingham Club, London.
Winner: G. Nigel Aspinall.
Runner-Up: A.B. Hope.

MISCELLANEOUS 1976 RESULTS

Palm Beach Invitational:
Held January 21-24 at Palm Beach, Florida.
Winners: Jack Osborn, New York and S. Joseph Tankoos, also of New York.
Runners-Up: John Young, Jr., Bermuda and Walter P. Margulies, Westhampton Beach, L.I., N.Y.

Eastern Seaboard Singles Championship "Doc Holden Trophy:"
Held March 18-20 at Palm Beach, Florida
Winner: Archie Peck, Palm Beach
Runner-Up: Jack Osborn, New York.

Bellows Cup Doubles Team Championship:
Held March 20-21, Palm Beach, Florida.
Winner: Palm Beach Croquet Club.
Runner-Up: New York Croquet Club.

ROQUE CLUBS

Arvin Roque Club
745 Third Avenue
Arvin, Texas

Barrington Area Roque Club
303 West Main
Barrington, Illinois

Clinton Roque Club
521 North Mulberry
Clinton, Illinois 61727

Dallas Roque Club
5439 Vanderbilt Avenue
Dallas, Texas

Decatur Roque Club
Fairview Park
Decatur, Illinois

Eastland Roque Club
410 North Walnut
Eastland, Texas 76448

Jefferson Roque Club
500 Jefferson Building
Houston, Texas 77001

Long Beach Roque Club
Lincoln Park
Long Beach, California

Los Angeles Roque Club
Exposition Park
Los Angeles, California

Lubbock Roque Club
MacKenzie State Park
Lubbock, Texas

Orlando Roque Club
915 Broadman Street
Orlando, Florida

Portage Path Croquet Club
425 North Portage Path
Akron, Ohio 44303

Redlands Roque Club
623 East Cypress Avenue
Redlands, California

Rock Creek Roque Club
3003 South Norton
Independence, Missouri 64052

Sunshine Roque Club
Mirror Lake Park
St. Petersburg, Florida

Two-Ball Association
c/o Bixby Park Roque Club
130 Cherry Avenue
Long Beach, California 90803

Wichita Roque Club
Linwood Park
Wichita, Kansas

All roque clubs under the aegis of:
American Roque League, Inc.
4205 Briar Creek Lane
Dallas, Texas 75214

UNITED STATES ROQUE CHAMPIONS

1882: A.G. Shipman, New York.
1883: G.W. Johnson, Philadelphia.
1884: George Harland, Norwich, Conn.
1885: Charles Jacobs, Springfield, Conn.
1886: A. Hull, Botsford, N.Y.
1887: A. Wambold, Staten Island.
1888: W.L. Bishop, Norwich, Conn.
1889: W.J. Johnson, Philadelphia.
1890: G.C. Strong, New London.
1891: Charles Smith, Martha's Vineyard.
1892: G.W. Johnson, Philadelphia.
1893: William Knecht, Matawan, N.J.
1894: G.C. Strong, New London.
1895: G.C. Strong, New London.
1896: Earl C. Butler, Middletown, Conn.
1897: Sacket L. Duryea, Washington, D.C.
1898: [NO CHAMPION].
1899: Charles W. Williams, Washington, D.C.
1900: Charles W. Williams, Washington, D.C.
1901: William M. Wahly, Washington, D.C.
1902: Sacket L. Duryea, Washington, D.C.
1903: Charles L. Cox, Malden, Mass.
1904: Charles L. Cox, Malden, Mass.
1905: Charles L. Cox, Malden, Mass.
1906: Clifford Howard, Washington, D.C.
1907: Herrold Bosworth, New London.
1908: Ed Clark, Springfield, Mass.
1909: Herrold Bosworth, N. London.
1910: Herrold Bosworth, N. London.
1911: Ed Clark, Springfield, Mass.
1912: Ed Clark, Springfield, Mass.

1913: E. Robinson, Mansfield, Mass.
1914: Ed Clark, Springfield, Mass.
1915: Herrold Bosworth, N. London.
1916: Herrold Bosworth, N. London.
1917: J.C. Kirk, Philadelphia.
1918: Charles Williams, Washington.
1919: Ed Clark, Springfield, Mass.
1920: F.C. Turner, Pasadena, Cal.
1921: Herbert Sime, Chicago, Ill.
1922: James Keane, Chicago, Ill.
1923: Herbert Sime, Chicago, Ill.
1924: W.W. Wilson, Chicago, Ill.
1925: A.S. Downey, Long Beach, Cal.
1926: A.G. Buffum, Los Angeles, Cal.
1927: O.E. Barnhart, Chicago, Ill.
1928: H.C. Haydon, Cleveland, Ohio.
1929: H.L. Smith, Pasadena, Cal.
1930: O.E. Barnhart, Chicago, Ill.
1931: Kenneth Moore, New Paris, Ohio.
1932: Ed Clark, Springfield, Mass.
1933: Frank Krause, Pasadena, Cal.
1934: O.E. Barnhart, Chicago, Ill.
1935: O.E. Barnhart, Chicago, Ill.
1936: Phil Wolf, Bellevue, Ohio.
1937: George Atkinson, Indianapolis.
1938: Wallace Martin, Waco, Texas.
1939: W.B. Reed, Fort Worth, Texas.
1940: C.E. Willis, Abilene, Texas.
1941: Pat Winton, Greenville, Texas.
1942-1945: [NO COMPETITION].
1946: Joe T. Bobbit, Hillsboro, Tex.
1947: F.B. Krause, Long Beach, Cal.
1948: F.B. Krause, Long Beach, Cal.

1949: F.B. Krause, Long Beach, Cal.
1950: E.W. Maddiex, Chicago, Ill.
1951: Bobby Arnold, Glendale, Cal.
1952: Arm G. Kapigian, Glendale, Cal.
1953: Arm G. Kapigian, Glendale, Cal.
1954: Bobby Arnold, Los Angeles.
1955: B.C. McGowan, Dallas and Merle Parker, Wichita, Kans.
1956: Bobby Arnold, Los Angeles, Cal.
1957: Bobby Arnold, Los Angeles, Cal.
1958: Bobby Arnold, Los Angeles, Cal.
1959: Arm G. Kapigian, Glendale, Cal.
1960: Bobby Arnold, Los Angeles.
1961: Wayne Stephens, Lubbock, Tex.

1962: Wayne Stephens, Lubbock, Tex.
1963: Wayne Stephens, Lubbock, Tex.
1964: Wayne Stephens, Lubbock, Tex.
1965: Tom Puryear, Greenville, Tex.
1966: Wayne Stephens, Lubbock, Tex.
1967: Tom Puryear, Greenville, Tex.
1968: Wayne Stephens, Lubbock, Tex.
1969: Bobby Arnold, Los Angeles.
1970: Wayne Stephens, Lubbock, Tex.
1971: Jack Green, Long Beach, Cal.
1972: Jack Green, Long Beach, Cal.
1973: C.B. Smith, Decatur, Ill.
1974: Jack Green, Long Beach, Cal.
1975: Jack Green, Long Beach, Cal.

Wayne Stephens and Bobby Arnold have each won seven titles; Ed Clark with six, also accomplished the feat of winning his last two championships thirteen years apart.

SUPPLIERS
OF CROQUET AND ROQUE EQUIPMENT

John Jaques and Sons, Ltd.
361 White Horse Road
Thornton Heath, Surrey
England

John Waterer, Sons and Crisp, Ltd.
Croquet Lawn Building and Maintenance
The Floral Mile
Twyford, Reading
England RG 10

Abercrombie and Fitch
Madison Avenue and 44th Street
New York, N.Y.

Lilliwhite's
Southampton, L.I., N.Y.

Stowe-Woodward, Inc.
4205 Briar Creek Lane
Dallas, Texas
(Manufacturers of Paralite roque balls).

Horchow Sports Collection
P.O. Box 34257
Dallas, Texas

Indiana Handle Company
Foley, Indiana

McGowan's Texas Sure Shot
4205 Briar Creek Lane
Dallas, Texas
(Manufacturer of roque equipment).

Melbourne Sports Depot
121 Elizabeth Street
Melbourne, Australia
(Suppliers of Jaques and M.S. Windsor mallets and gear).

Action Sportswear
Specialists, Pty. Ltd.
Edments Building 7th Floor
38 Gawler Place
Adelaide, Australia

Bert Oldfield's Sports Store
243 Pitt Street
Sydney, Australia
(Suppliers of Jaques and Oliver).

Ron Marks
17 Elizabeth Street
Melbourne, Australia
(Trophies, club hat bands, accessories, jewelry).

South Bend Toy Company
200 5th Avenue
New York, N.Y.

Forsters Manufacturing Co.
Depot Street
Wilton, Maine

Bibliography

General Works:

American Roque League, Inc.: *Roque: The Game of the Century.* Dallas, 1975.

Brown, Paul: *Croquet: Rules and Strategy for Home Play.* D. Van Nostrand & Co. New York, 1957.

Carroll, Lewis: *Alice's Adventures In Wonderland.* New American Library of World Literature, Inc.. New York, 1960.

Champ, Paul: *Lawn Tennis, Golf, Croquet, Polo.* 1911.

Cotter, E.P.C.: *Tackle Croquet This Way.* Stanley Paul. London, 1960.

Croquet Association: *The Laws of Association Croquet and Golf Croquet & The Regulations For Tournaments.* London, 1972.

Croquet Association: *Handbook On Modern Croquet.* Longmans Green & Co.. London, 1931.

Crowther-Smith, H.F.: *The Art of Croquet: A Practical Handbook.* H., F., & G. Witherby. London, 1932.

Donaldson, Dorothy: in *World Book Encyclopedia.* Field Enterprises Educational Corporation. Chicago, 1961.

Elvey, Rev. G.F. Handel: *Croquet (Association Croquet): A Handbook On the Strokes & Tactics of the Game.* John Jaques & Son, Ltd. Surrey, 1949.

Gommes, Alice B.: *Traditional Games of England, Scotland and Ireland,* Vol. 1. Dover Publications. New York, 1964.

Heath, James Dunbar: *Complete Croquet Player.* Routelege & Son. London, 1896.

Jacobus, Charles: *Croquet and Its Rules.* American Sports Publications. New York, 1907.

Jaques, John: *Croquet: Laws and Regulations of the Game.* A. Williams, 1865.

Lauthier, Joseph: *New Rules For the Game of Mail.* Paris, 1910.

Locock, C.D.: *Modern Croquet Tactics.* 1907.

Longman, William: *Croquet In the 60's.* London, 1921.

Marx, Harpo and Barber, Roland: *Harpo Speaks.* Freeway Press, Inc.. New York, 1974

McGowan, B.C.: *By-Laws, Rules and Regulations of the Two-Ball and Royal Roque.* American Roque League, Inc.. Dallas, 1957.

Menke, Frank G.: *Encyclopedia of Sports.* A.S. Barnes & Co.. New York, 1953.

Miller, David and Thorp, Rupert: *Croquet and How To Play It.* Faber and Faber. London, 1966.

Nabokov, Vladimir: *Pnin.* Avon Books. New York, 1953.

National Croquet Association, Inc.: *Croquet.* Oklahoma City, 1963.

Omerod, Dr. G.I.: *Know the Game: Croquet.* Educational Productions, Ltd.. Yorkshire, 1971.

Perkes, Dan: *Official Associated Press Sports Almanac.* Dell Publishing Co.. New York, 1975.

Prior, Richard Chandler Alexander: *Notes on Croquet and Some Ancient Bat and Ball Games Related To It.* London, 1872.

Reckitt, Maurice Benington: *Croquet Today.* McDonald. London, 1954.

Reckitt, Maurice Benington *et. al.*: in *Encyclopedia Brittanica.* Encyclopedia Brittanica Inc.. Chicago, 1964.

Reid, Captain Mayne A.: *Croquet: A Treatise With Notes and Commentary.* Publishing Office of 119 Nassau Street. New York, 1869.

Ross, Arthur G.: *Croquet and How To Play It*. Wellington, Wedderspoon & Co.. London, 1947.

Ross, Arthur G.: *Croquet Handbook*. Nicholas Kaye. London, 1959.

Routelege, Edmund: *Beadles' Dime Handbook of Croquet*. New York, 1866.

Rover, A.: *Croquet: Its Principles and Rules*. M. Bradley & Co.. Springfield, 1871. 13th Edition

Schultz, Nikki: *Backyard Games*. Grosset & Dunlap. New York, 1975.

Scudder, Horace Elisha: *The Game of Croquet: Its Appointments and Laws*. Hurd & Houghton, 1865.

Solomon, J.W.: *Croquet*. B.T. Batford. London, 1966.

Teichmann, Howard: *George S. Kaufman: An Intimate Biography*. Atheneum Books. New York, 1972.

Tollemache, Bentley Lyonel John: *Croquet By Lord Tollemache*. S. Paul. London, 1914.

Wells, H.G.: *The Croquet Player: A Story*. N.C.W. Viking. New York, 1937.

Whipple, G.M. and Smith, A.A.: *Croquet: Rules and Regulations*. Salem, 1871.

Williams, L.B.: *Croquet*. A.D. Innes & Co.. London, 1899.

[Anonymous]: *Croquet As Played By the Newport Croquet Club*. Sheldon & Co.. New York, 1867.

Periodicals:

Hart, Moss: 'East-West Croquet.' *Life,* July 22, 1946.

Jenks, Tudor: 'Antiquarian Athletics.' *Outing,* January 1909.

Maas, Peter: 'Sport of Stings.' *Holiday,* October 1967.

MacKenzie, Sir Compton: 'Croquet: The Ideal Pastime.' *Spectator,* July 2, 1954.

Mallalieu, J.P.W.: 'Perfection on the Lawn.' *Spectator,* July 17, 1953.

Mathus, K.: 'Croquet Tips.' *Popular Science,* August 1945.

Mathewson, Joseph: 'Right Out Of Their League.' *Sports Illustrated,* April 5, 1971.

Olszewska, E.S. and Ross, Alan S.C.: 'Hong Kong In Croquet.' *Notes & Queries,* September 1965.

Ross, Alan S.C.: 'Croquet.' *Notes & Queries,* August 1968.

Australian Croquet Council Gazette, April, 1975.

'Awfully Good Show.' *Time,* July 31, 1950.

'Croquet.' *Canada,* June 1921.

'Croquet At Eighty-Two: With Rules Adopted At Louisville, Kentucky.' *Recreation,* March 1936.

'Croquet: Favorite Form of Recreation.' *Recreation,* July 1948.

'Croquet Golf.' *Playground,* November 1929.

'Croquet Golf Courses on Playgrounds.' *Recreation,* March 1931.

'Croquet Is For Everyone.' *Popular Gardener,* March 1966.

'Croquet Lives.' *Newsweek,* July 30, 1973.

'Croquet: Social Shock Absorber.' *Arts and Decoration,* August 1932.

'Cue Roque Table.' *Industrial Arts,* January 1929.

'Figure Croquet Wickets Of Sheet Metal Are Quite Easily Seen.' *Popular Mechanics,* May 1941.

'In the Days Of Croquet.' *Freeman,* May 30, 1923.

'Lawn Bowlers' Controversy.' New York *Times,* May 4, 1972.

Life, November 15, 1948.

'Mallets Across the Blinkin' Sea.' *Sports Illustrated,* July 31, 1967.
'Mallet Men Of Manhattan.' *Christian Science,* October 1937.
'New Croquet Roque.' *Collier's,* August 12, 1911.
'Outdoor Recreation At Night.' *Suburban Life,* August 1907.
Picture Post, May 27, 1939.
'Roque As A Suburban Pastime.' *Suburban Life,* March 1911.
'Roque: Modern Croquet.' *Outing,* September 1901.
Spectator, June 11, 1953.
Sports Illustrated, January 30, 1956.
Sports Illustrated, August 30, 1954.
'Sticky Wicket.' *Newsweek,* August 29, 1966.